GAME, SET, LIFE

WAYNE J. STREET, JR.

GAME, SET, LIFE

MY MATCH WITH CROHN'S AND CANCER

Tate Publishing & Enterprises

Published by Tate Publishing & Enterprises, LLC
127 E. Trade Center Terrace | Mustang, Oklahoma 73064 USA
1.888.361.9473 | www.tatepublishing.com

Tate Publishing is committed to excellence in the publishing industry. The company reflects the philosophy established by the founders, based on Psalm 68:11,
"The Lord gave the word and great was the company of those who published it."

Book design copyright © 2009 by Tate Publishing, LLC. All rights reserved.
Cover design by Tyler Evans
Interior design by Jeff Fisher

Published in the United States of America

ISBN: 978-1-61566-260-9
1. Biography & Autobiography, Personal Memoirs
2. Self-Help, Motivational & Inspirational
09.10.12

For Tiffany and William.
I'll love you forever!

ACKNOWLEDGMENTS

My story wouldn't have been possible without the many people who have helped me out. I've been blessed to have had so many people in my life.

To my writing network: Marlene, your suggestions, patience, and ideas kept me moving along. And to the ladies in our writing group—Margo, Michelle, and Susan—thanks. Your comments and suggestions have helped me shape this into something special. Deborah, thank you for sharing your passion for writing with me and challenging me to pursue this project. And to Nick, thank you for your encouragement; without it, this would still be just an idea. Derka, Derka. And to Steve Stedman, my teacher, my colleague and my friend: Thanks for taking the time to proofread my very, very rough draft.

To my medical team: Dr Robert Myers, you gave me answers and hope when no one else could. Dr. Jeffrey Fox, thank you for continuing the care that Dr. Myers began to provide. To Dr. Pryor you said you would be dragging me through the mud, which you certainly did. Thanks for pulling me out of it in the end. And to my nurses at Kaiser: Thanks for treating me. Despite all of the needle sticks, I keep coming back.

To my running buddies, Keith and Kim; I have enjoyed every mile of it. Well, almost every mile of it.

Thank you, Rob and Martha, for all you've done for me and my family. And to the rest of my PVAC family: The friendships, the experiences, the memories, and the bonds that we have created will last a lifetime.

Chris Oakes and Izzy Derkos: You have been my best teachers.

John, Lori, Katie, Izzy, and Madilyn: Thanks for opening your home and hearts to me, Tiffany, and George. Thanks for being family. We love you very much.

To my mother, Carol, and father, Wayne Sr.: Thank you for teaching me between right and wrong, loving me, and giving me every opportunity to succeed. P.S. Mom, thank you for making me do all of those things I never wanted to do.

To my six siblings: Steve, Katee, Beth, Bobby, Mike, and Pat. Life without a big family would be boring. I love you all.

To my beautiful wife, Tiffany, for giving me love, trust, and compassion, and for giving me the greatest gift I could ever imagine—our son, William.

CHAPTER 1

*Who says that love means
nothing to a tennis player?*

AS A CHILD, I WAS painfully shy. I clung to my father's leg most every waking moment, rarely letting go without a fight. My mother could retell stories of my daily ritual as I stood in the front window of our home, crying as my father drove off to work. I would swear each day that he was never going to come back. But at the end of each day, he did.

I never spoke more than a word or two to anyone other than my immediate family until I was five years old. Our neighbor, Mr. Miller, came over to help my father move a large piece of furniture. I walked right up to him, said hello, and just as quickly as I entered the room, I left.

My father would later recall that incident fondly, smiling and reiterating Mr. Miller's response: "I didn't figure that boy of yours was ever going to talk." My father just smiled and said, "I figured about the same thing."

As I grew, so did my shyness. I wanted to stay at home and hover close to my parent's legs, shying away from new people, and expressed a genuine fear of trying new things.

I remember how devastated I was when my mother said, "Junior, you are going to play soccer this year." At the age of seven, just the very thought of having to be out on the field with so many others petrified me. I ended up playing eight seasons of youth soccer and loved every minute.

I protested again when at the age of fifteen, my mother suggested that I go to tennis camp during the summer. Against my wishes, I went. Today, I reflected on my refusal and just laugh. I'm grateful that she dragged me to soccer, tennis camp, and the many other activities that I told her I was not going to do.

AT THE END OF THE third grade, my parents signed up for a family membership at the local gym. My mom wanted a safe place for me and my siblings to learn how to swim and be active. My mother knew that I needed to get more active. To put it mildly, I was a bit portly. I was a very thick and heavyset boy for my age all the way up through my senior year of high school.

Over the course of the fourth-grade school year, my mother brought me and my siblings down to the club to swim and release our excess energies. When we got bored of swimming, my mom and I tried something new: racquetball.

My mother said to me one day, "Junior, let's go to the library and find a book about the game."

I agreed, so we went to the library one rainy afternoon and checked out three different books on racquetball.

"Won't we need racquets too?" I asked. Without saying a word, we went straight to Kmart to find a couple of racquets.

Neither of us was very good at the game, as I can recall. My mother was able to beat me more than I could her. I struggled learning the game but kept on it at Mom's urging. As the school year progressed, the fall had turned into winter, so the weather was more conducive to racquetball than anything else I continued to play. My game, though, did not progress.

I was at heightened frustration with my game, to say the least. "I am not getting any better," I would exclaim to my mother.

She would just blurt back, "Well, you are just going to have to try a little harder." I always hated when she would do that. She knew me well enough to know that I would try again and again and again.

My patience for the cursed game of racquetball began to run thin: I don't know how many days I caught myself staring outside to the other set of courts that the facility had—tennis courts. They seemed so vast and far out there. It was such a foreign game to me. I had seen it on television; however, I had interest in learning about it.

Maybe it was because of the strange scoring. One moment, it was 15–15. Then the next minute it was 30–15. *Why did they skip all of those other points?* My ten-year-old mind would ask itself. I had a difficult time trying to following the strange scoring.

BEING OUTSIDE WAS REALLY APPEALING to me, though. Racquet-ball had been fun, but I really had no interest in staying indoors trying to hit a ball against a wall when I could be playing outside.

I think my mother had sensed that too. We were missing out on the sunlight.

Then one summer day my mother asked me, "How about we try tennis, Junior?"

"Really?" I asked excitedly, "When can we start?"

"Right now," she replied. And once again, we trekked to the library to find a book about tennis, and then back Kmart to get equipped. "This is going to be such great fun," she would declare. "Aren't you excited?" I smiled.

Later that afternoon, we took our first trip to the tennis courts.

Today, when I think of our first trip to the courts, I realize how fateful it was. My mother and I started to play just to have something to do. Twenty years later, it is a safe bet that if you need to find one or both of us, just come down to the tennis club and look out to the seven courts.

Now the sport defines me. It is who I am. It's my greatest passion.

My tennis experience has been a journey not a destination. And like many individuals who embark down a new and unknown road, it has been scary from time to time because there hasn't always been a destination in sight.

So many of my life experiences have revolved around tennis, both on and off of the court; I've had two wonderful coaches for role models who taught me more than just the silly game of tennis.

I've befriended many great people through the sport, many with whom my relationships have transcended the tennis courts.

And little did I know that I would meet my future wife at a tennis match. Who says that love means nothing to a tennis player?

Then there was that day when I was watching a tennis match and everything changed.

TODAY, I AM STILL PLAYING tennis, though not as much as I would like. My teaching career, my wife and my young son take up the bulk of my time. It's a delicate balance to squeeze my life into a twenty-four hour day but I manage. As a teacher, the only thing that could rival my enjoyment for tennis might be the first day of summer vacation.

CHAPTER 2

Alas, the first day of summer was here.

THE FIRST DAY OF SUMMER vacation is precious—no, sacred—to this tired teacher. I was alone at last. My wife and four-month-old son, William, headed out of town for the day around mid-morning as part of their weekly trip to her parents', who lived a couple towns over.

And the most important task on my list of "things to do today" was a nice, long, peaceful afternoon nap on my couch.

Another hard, long, and taxing school year had just ended for this veteran social studies teacher. All I wanted, and what I needed, was a little bit of sacred alone time to decompress from the year.

As I worked around the house that morning, cleaning the floors, wiping out the sink, and several other not-so-fun chores, I remained acutely aware that the completion of each task brought me one step closer to my well-deserved afternoon nap.

My thoughts wandered as I worked. When I was knee-deep in grime while cleaning the floor, I began to think about many of the highs and lows of the past school year. *What went well? I should have done that project. I wish I had more time for that unit.* The reflections of the school year filled my mind.

By early afternoon, I reached the end of my list. I was ready for sleep. I knew that if I didn't hit the pillow soon that this nap would never happen. There was only a small window of time for the most restful nap, and I wasn't going to let it close on me. I crashed down onto the couch for my hard-earned rest, closed my eyes, and smiled. Bliss! I could take this and be assured of a quiet and peaceful rest with no interruptions.

I started to drift off into a deep slumber when the distinct rapping of knuckles began knocking on my front door, threatening to ruin my nap. I leapt from the couch, reacting to the sudden intrusion to my peace and quiet. Annoyed by the interruption, I approached the door. Peering through the spy hole out of habit, I saw…*my neighbor, in his god-awful Hawaiian shirt.*

I opened the door to a, "Hey, neighbor, can I bum a couple of matches off you for the barby?" followed up by a chuckle that was way too energetic for me. I retrieved a handful of my long, stick matches for him from the kitchen and said good-bye very groggily as I shut the door before heading back to my continued pursuit of the coveted nap.

As I lay down again on the couch, my body was becoming overwhelmed by sleep and a great sense of relief. I was greatly relieved for the quiet again. I was relieved that I didn't need to do any more lesson planning. I was relieved that there were no more papers to grade. And I was relieved that all of the shenanigans that revolved around my job were over for the next twelve whole weeks.

Letting all of those thoughts go allowed me to unwind. I could feel my body begin to relax. I can recall that it wasn't too long ago that I was inundated with the continuous responsibilities of lesson planning, grading, correcting, collaborating with other teachers, participating with PLCs, SLCs, IEPs, Clusters (among other teacher acronyms) and interacting with parents. And it wasn't too long ago when I thought that I would never see this first day of summer. With each deep exhalation I took, I could feel all of the anxieties of the school year getting blown away, and I was out.

Alas, the first day of summer was here.

Another knock! This knock was a distinguished sound. Opening my eyes, I looked around, but I was no longer on my couch. I was seated in a chair in front of an oak desk. Another knock at the door rattled my eardrums. I swiveled in my chair to see that this time it wasn't my neighbor but a man in a long, white coat. As he entered the room, he took his seat across from me, setting a file folder on his desktop, neatly in line with all of the others.

"Hello, Junior," he said looking me straight in the

eyes. There was a long pause. He made himself comfortable, pulling himself toward the edge of the desk. His chair squeaked as he reached across his desk for one of the other file folders. "I've been reading through your file."

He sat up as he opened the folder and glanced at it briefly before setting it back in line with all of the others. "Junior, you're dying."

"No! No!" I shouted. Jumping out of my chair, I felt a sudden pain in my gut. I hunched over, placing my left hand on the wall for support. Dazed, I tried to catch my breath. I began to choke. My knees buckled.

"Doc, say it ain't so." I looked him in the eye and begged, "Say it ain't so, Doc." I slumped back in my chair.

Another loud knock at the door shook me up as I heard a distressed voice say, "Junior, hurry. I can't hold this any longer. Help me, hurry!"

I opened my eyes and sprang from the couch. I looked around the room. *No oak desk, no white coat, no file folders.* I took another deep breath. *Thank God. It was only a dream.*

"Junior, I need help now," the voice behind the door begged.

I stumbled to the door and looked through the spy hole to see my wife and son.

Smiling, I opened the door wide and greeted my lovely wife. Her arms were full. The diaper bag was draped over her shoulder, groceries in one arm, and William in the other. I reached out to grab the groceries just as the bag split down the side, spilling the tomatoes and canned goods all over the porch. We looked at each other and just laughed. "I'll get them," I said as my wife walked past me and into the house.

I stepped out onto the porch to clean up the mess. As I got down on my hands and knees to pick up the groceries, I smiled. I smiled, realizing that my nap and quiet afternoon were over. I smiled knowing that the day and nap provided me with a feeling of accomplishment and satisfaction. I smiled because I could start looking forward to my second day of summer vacation. I smiled because my loving wife and precious, handsome son were back at home with me. Lastly, I smiled in relief because I knew that there were numerous occasions in the past fourteen years in which I thought that I might never see this first day of summer.

CHAPTER 3

Three days. That was the rule.

MY MOTHER'S ATTITUDE WAS QUITE simple. Three days. That was the rule. Unless one of us kids were bleeding or dying, three days was the required wait time before she would consider taking us to the doctors. Mom wouldn't have it any other way.

I can still hear her voice. "You really aren't sick, honey, unless you've had that cold for more than three days."

Inevitably, one of us would try and protest to no avail.

"You're getting dressed and going to school." Smiling, she'd send us out the door and say to us reassuringly, "If you don't feel better in three days, I will call the doctor. I promise." She ended it with a loving kiss on the cheek and a gentle pat on the back as we went out the door.

Mom was a protective parent but never hovered. With seven children, it was impractical to rush to the doctor's office whenever a medical issue arose, so we waited. If she had rushed us to the doctor's office with every scrape, break, or illness, she could've had her own parking spot at the doctor's. The three days would often come and go, along with the ailment that had afflicted us so grievously. *Sheer genius, Mom!*

We did have our fair share of medical concerns. Because we were an active bunch, we had numerous sprains and breaks. My older brother had an arm in a sling several times while my sisters each suffered from ankle sprains. There was nothing, though, that a little bit of time and our mother's love wouldn't heal.

We weren't immune from the cold and flu season either. It was a vicious cycle once it started. Everyone caught it in some form or another. No two people ever seemed to have it at the same time. It might've started with my older brother and then on to my mother, who somehow passed it on to one of my baby brothers. And the illness would go on.

On the other hand my father and I were very fortunate. We always managed to exit the flu season unscathed. To the best of my recollection, my dad, in forty-one years of teaching first grade, only missed one day of school due to any illness.

We were quite blessed; no life-threatening illnesses, and no surgeries. Just some scrapes, bruises, stitches, broken bones, and flu—until my senior year of high school; then our luck changed.

MY AUTUMNAL SUNDAYS WERE SPENT doing three activities: church, tennis, and watching football. It was mid-October, and I found myself in front of the television one early Sunday afternoon suffering through another Oakland Raider debacle. They could have used all of my prayers that afternoon. At the two-minute warning commercial break, I had the sudden and unusually powerful urge to use the bathroom. I hustled off the family couch and down the stairs to the bathroom, genuinely concerned that I might not make it in time. Luckily, I did.

When I was finished, I stood up, pulled up my shorts, and, out of force of habit, I spat into the toilet bowl. That's when I first saw it: blood!

That's odd. I haven't seen anything like that before. I leaned in a little closer for a better look. There was a hint of red on some of the toilet paper, along with a tinge of blood throughout the entire bowl. I even examined my boxer shorts to discover a light streak of red. I wasn't sure what to do or how concerned I should be. I thought about it for a second and then flushed the toilet. I cleaned up and returned to the Raiders game, wanting to forget all about the blood.

As the game dragged on, my stomach began to ache more. I concluded that it was from the poor play of the Raiders, but as the afternoon progressed, so did the discomfort in my belly and the frequency of my trips to the bathroom.

This ache was different from what I had ever had before. This pain left me doubled over on the couch. I struggled to reposition my legs and torso again and again to try and find an elusively comfortable position. I gingerly curled my legs into a fetal position that allowed the cramping to subside for a few minutes at a time. I would start to get comfortable, and there would be another cramp that would send me reeling in pain. *Wow. This might be a while before I get better.*

As dinner approached, I told my mother, "I don't feel so well. I think I'm going to skip dinner and lay down for a while in my room."

"Are you sure?" she asked. "I can bring you something. Soup or crackers?"

"No thanks. I'll be fine."

"Okay, dear," she said. "Let me know if I can get you something later. Promise?" she asked.

"All right," I shut the door behind me after I entered my room. I planned on taking a few minutes to gather up my schoolbooks and school clothes for the next day; then I thought I would be able to get to sleep a little earlier than usual.

I climbed into bed and pulled the covers up to my chin. As I rolled over on to my side, I prayed that I could fall asleep. *Please God, make this pain go away.* I prayed for a long, healthy sleep to help alleviate my discomfort. I closed my eyes and tried to assure myself that it would be better tomorrow.

It wasn't. The next day, the bleeding was still occurring at each bathroom visit. The cramping wasn't as bad; it had subsided a bit, which allowed me to sit up right at my desk—*at least for the time being.*

I ended up leaving trigonometry class three times

during first period to go to the bathroom. And each time, I dreaded it; *school bathrooms, disgusting.*

By lunchtime, I was overwhelmed. I ended up spending my lunch hour in a bathroom stall. I was beginning to panic. This type of rectal bleeding wasn't something I wanted to talk to my friends about. *What might they say?* And I was too embarrassed to talk to anyone in my family, especially my parents. I was a shy, self-conscious teenage boy. So I did what first came to mind. *Wait three days and see what happens.*

The three days came and went—slowly. I was both embarrassed about people finding out about my bottom bleeding and scared to death to know why it was bleeding. I tried to follow my daily routine of school, tennis, and my after-school job, but the sudden bowel movements were proving this to be too difficult.

As the fall progressed, so did my illness. My weight dropped from a robust 210 pounds to a paltry 150 pounds. I hid the weight loss by layering my clothes: a t-shirt; then a button-down shirt; then a sweatshirt; and, as it got colder, a light jacket on top of all that. It must have worked because Mom didn't ask about my weight loss. But when I began to have difficulty tipping the scales at 150, I knew that I was in trouble. My 6'1" frame needed more beef to it. I figured I was running out of time before Mom would start asking questions that I couldn't or didn't want to answer.

The bleeding continued, and to my dismay, my bowel movements became more frequent. Two times a day became five times a day; then five times an hour; and at the zenith, I was in the bathroom up to twenty or twenty-five times in a single day. My cheeks were raw. No one in my family seemed to notice all of my trips to the bathroom. I assumed they were all too busy with their own lives.

My illness was forcing me to change my life. I began to stay home and avoid activities that might keep me away from a quick, convenient and above all clean bathroom. One weekend in late November, I missed out on the big game between the University of California and Stanford. My friends and family went every year. I hated to miss out, but I knew there was no way I could go without having an accident. I grabbed my history textbook and plopped down on the bed.

As I started to read, the door opened. Mom popped her head in, "Are you feeling all right?"

"Yeah, Mom. I'm fine," I lied.

"Okay. I just thought I'd ask." She continued. "You just don't quite seem like yourself lately."

"I just have a lot on my mind, Mom. That's all."

"Yeah. You're right," she said. "You have been busy, haven't you? Well, have a good day, and don't study too hard." She shot me a smile and then left my room.

I closed my book and thought about her question. *Are you feeling all right?* Her question was my first indicator that she was suspicious of something. I thought I was so smart hiding my symptoms from her, hiding the fact that I didn't feel normal. I suspect she let me be because I didn't complain. After all, I knew she always had enough to think about with her teaching job and six other kids to take care of.

My worst attack occurred on the tennis courts a

couple of days after the big game. I was trying my best to keep up with my friend, Ross. Normally, our intense rivalry made me a better player, but that day, my feet dragged, and I lacked my usual hustle. I struggled to keep up. After the first set, we took a break before changing ends of the court.

Ross asked me, "Junior, everything okay?"

"Sure it is."

"Really?" he asked. "You just don't seem to be yourself out here on the court."

"I guess I'm just not moving my feet too well. That's all." I took another sip of Gatorade from my bottle and said, "I must not be watching the ball too well either."

Seeming satisfied, he set down his water, and we marched off to opposite ends of the court like two gentlemen about to duel. It was his turn to serve. As he called out the score—"Second set,"—I dropped my racquet and doubled over in pain resting on my hands and knees trying to get comfortable.

"Junior, what happened?" he asked as he ran across the court to my side.

I made an effort to get up with his assistance. "It is just a really bad cramp." I had leaned over again in pain. "I'm sorry. I've got to stop." I reached to pick up my racquet, and then it hit me, the uncontrollable urge of a bowel movement. "Oh no, Ross. I gotta go to the bathroom." I grabbed my backpack as I sprinted off the court to the bathroom, trying to avoid an embarrassing incident. And for the first time since the symptoms began, I had an accident in my shorts.

Unnoticed by others around the courts, I made it to the bathroom and locked the door behind me. I was a mess. It was everywhere: down my legs, on my calves, in my shorts, and on my shoes. I didn't know what to do. For the first time, my entire feelings came to a head, and I cried. I cried because I was embarrassed. I cried because I was scared. I cried because I felt that I was losing control of my life. I was covered in crap, and tears were rolling down my face. A voice seeped into my consciousness.

"Junior, are you all right in there?"

Ross's voice snapped me from my crying. I took a deep breath and wiped a tear away; then I managed to answer, "I'll be out in a minute." I had to think quickly. *How am I going to make myself presentable?*

I searched through my backpack. *Good, an extra pair of shorts.* My mother had taught me to always carry extra clothing just in case anything ever happened. *I don't think that she anything like this in mind though.* It took about five minutes for me to get presentable enough to come out of the bathroom. I had wiped my legs off with a wet paper towel and finished by throwing away my shorts and underwear, burying them deep in the trash can with the hopes that they wouldn't be found.

I came out of the bathroom and saw Ross waiting with a smile. He asked, "Is everything all right?"

I needed to tell someone, and this presented me with a perfect opportunity. "No, it isn't." I told him everything. "I haven't been feeling well for several weeks now." I even mentioned what happened just moments before and in the bathroom.

He listened intently. When I was finished, he shrugged his shoulders and said, "Oh well, Junior. Shit happens."

We both laughed, and then he handed me my racquet from off the ground and said, "Let's get going! I'll give you a ride home."

"Thanks."

Together, we walked out of the club, both carrying our tennis gear and closely guarding my humiliating little secret.

THE INCIDENT WITH ROSS HAD given me the courage to open up. I thought I'd been so smart. I had tried to hide my embarrassment and mask the symptoms to no avail. Mom's three-day rule had been a very valuable lesson for me. It had taught me self-reliance and independence. Unfortunately, the three days' wait had turned into a month. All it had gotten me was isolation.

That night, after everyone had settled in for the evening, Dad was in his easy chair grading papers, my sister was finishing her homework in the living room, and my brothers were in the game room watching an episode of *The Simpsons*. I heard my brother's laugh as Homer said, "D'oh."

I entered the kitchen as my mom washed the dishes. I offered to dry the dishes. "Mom, I need to talk with you. I think something is seriously wrong with me."

"What is it, Junior?" she asked as she set down the dish she had in her hand.

"Well, I didn't want to worry you, so I waited three days." I lowered my voice and mumbled, "And maybe a month." My voice trailed away.

"What did you say?" Mom asked, "Did you say a month?"

I froze in panic.

"Yes," I said sheepishly. I looked away, afraid to make eye contact with her.

"A month?" she repeated. "What were you thinking?"

"I was embarrassed." I slumped my shoulders. "I thought it was the flu, but its not."

She dried off her hands and walked across the kitchen to me. I was uptight and afraid as to what she might do next. Sometimes I wasn't sure how she would react to big news. She hugged me. "I will call Dr. Levinthal in the morning." I was relieved.

"Okay," I replied. She felt my forehead for a temperature and then stepped back to take a good look at me up and down.

"Now go right to bed," she said, spinning me around toward my room. "No school for you tomorrow." I looked back at her with a raised eyebrow. *No school?* I knew she was concerned when she said I was staying home.

I lay down in bed shortly thereafter, relieved that I finally shared my burden with someone and relieved that my mother was calling Dr. Levinthal in the morning. *Dr. Levinthal always makes me feel better.*

The next morning, I awoke a little after ten in the morning. I came out of my room, and my mother was at work in the kitchen.

"Good morning, sleepy."

I wiped my eyes. "Good morning," I said groggily.

"Are you feeling any better?"

I shrugged my shoulders. "So far."

"Good. Well, I called the doctor. She is out all week. I forgot that this week is Thanksgiving. I got you an appointment next Monday."

"So what should we do until then?" I asked.

"We wait and relax," she stated, "and we will rest. Go watch some television and I will get you something to eat. After all, you're not the only one who's been worried about you lately." With that, she walked back up into the kitchen to get me some food.

I sat on the couch stunned. *How on earth did she know?* I realized at that moment that my mother was wiser and more aware of everything going on around her than she had ever let on.

Moments later, she came out of the kitchen with a bowl of fruit and a glass of juice. "Here you are, honey. Is there anything else that I can do for you?"

"No, thank you," I replied. "This is great. Thanks."

"I am going to the grocery store." She held up her list. "I need to get some last-minute items for Thanksgiving."

"Okay, Mom." I pointed to my seat. "I'll be right here," I paused, "or maybe in the bathroom."

Mom walked back into the kitchen and came back over to the couch. "By the way, your senior pictures came the other day." She dropped them into my lap and gave me a kiss good-bye.

I sat there for a moment contemplating whether or not to look at them. Temptation got the best of me. I opened them up, and it hit me. The pictures showed a heavier, stronger person. I was smiling and beaming with life. It became suddenly obvious; the boy in the picture was not the same one sitting on the couch. I guess Mom figured that out a little sooner than me.

THANKSGIVING ARRIVED THREE DAYS LATER. Mom said all I had to do was lounge around all day and watch football. "I'll tell your brothers and sisters and cousins that you aren't feeling well and you need your rest."

"That sounds good to me," I told her with a half smile. I was too tired to offer her a full one.

Our annual Thanksgiving gathering proved, once again, to be quite the feast. The house was filled with about twenty-five family members. My dad interrupted my football watching once. He needed me to help him get the extra leaves in the table. Then it was back to the couch.

I tried to nap on the couch. I kept getting disrupted—aunts, uncles, and cousins. Each person disrupted me, unknowing that I was both trying to sleep and sick.

My mother was in the kitchen not only making a feast but creating noise as she dropped a pot on the floor and slammed a cupboard door shut.

There were intermittent bursts of laughter coming

from the family room as Uncle Bob started in with one of his famous stories. His stories were quite memorable because the stories usually involved my mother as a child in one of her many follies. He always seemed to be the hero of his story, and my mother was either the villain or the victim. *Funny how it always turned out that way.*

My siblings and cousins were running back and forth from the football game to the Nintendo or to the family room to catch part of the story from Uncle Bob.

Normally, I would be right in the middle of the action, but all I could do was fake a smile when someone looked my way. I tried to stay relaxed. I was in great pain as I tried to fight off the cramps and my grumbling bowels.

I was barely aware of all the fun I was missing out on all around me. I tried not to be jealous of all the fun that everyone else seemed to be having.

I always love our family holiday dinners. There is an energy that bounces around the table as the stories are shared and jokes are told. But that day, I was drained and couldn't harness any of the energy that was emanating from the table. I might catch the snippet of a story from Uncle Bob or the tail end of a joke from my cousin. When anyone looked my way, I would flash a halfhearted smile and laugh lethargically. My intense stomach pains drew my attentions away from the stories.

Nothing at the table looked appetizing, but I piled a couple of slices of turkey on my plate next to my mother's prized stuffing. I took a bite of stuffing; it had little taste. I set my fork back on my plate and leaned back in my chair. I took in the scene at the table as the entire family carried on. I felt that I went unnoticed. I gently and quietly pushed the plate away.

I reached out to take another bite; then it hit me. There was a sudden urge to go to the bathroom. I calmly stood up out of my seat, excusing myself to the restroom. I barely made it before my bowels exploded. *Diarrhea and blood again;* it had become the expected rather than the exception.

After a few minutes in the bathroom, I headed back from the bathroom and passed through the kitchen to get a glass of water. The table was still buzzing when I overheard my grandmother ask my mother, "Carol, what is wrong with Junior?"

"What do you mean, Mom?"

"Oh, come on, Carol. He is so skinny and pale. What is wrong?"

"I don't know." She hesitated. "He just hasn't been feeling to well lately."

"Well, he's too skinny. I liked it better when he was chubby."

"Mom, he was never chubby."

"Right, and I've never been short," Granny replied sarcastically.

I thought it was a good idea to break up that conversation before people started asking me any more questions. I re-entered the dining room and asked, "Does anyone need anything while I am up?"

Everyone declined, and I took my seat once more.

I looked across the table at Granny and Mom, and they had moved onto another topic. *Thank goodness.*

As dinner concluded, my mother began to bring out desserts. It was a cornucopia of goodies. Pie, cakes, cookies, and chocolate truffles; it all looked good, but my stomach was telling me that it all tasted terrible.

As we sat and ate our selected treats, I felt as if some of my cousins were starting to stare at me. I just looked down at my empty dessert plate trying to avoid eye contact. After watching my brother Mike take his third mouthful of pumpkin pie, I just couldn't stomach it any more.

I stood up from the table and said my good nights to everyone and walked off to my bedroom. I was relieved that the holiday was over for me. My stomach was on fire. The burning continued most of the night. Luckily, I was able to fade away into a restless sleep. It carried me through the night and into the next morning, when I would start the misery all over again.

IT WAS OUR FAMILY TRADITION to go to Larsen's Christmas Tree Farm the day after Thanksgiving. We would all gather into the family's faded, red station wagon, and one lucky person would get to ride in our dad's beat-up pickup. My little sister, Beth, usually led the way and always seemed to want the largest and most expensive tree that Mr. Larsen had to offer. That year was the first and only time I didn't go to the tree farm.

I was afraid to leave the house, concerned that I might have another accident in my shorts. The incident at the tennis courts was still very fresh in my mind. The previous night had been difficult. And since I had only managed a couple of hours of sleep. My energy had been sapped. I lay on the couch with the remote in hand, flipping back and forth between college football and the *Planet of the Apes* movie marathon.

I was depressed. With the most festive time of the year and my senior year as the backdrop of my life, I was miserable. I couldn't enjoy myself. I should have been out having fun. I should have been at the tree farm, fighting with my sister over the perfect tree. I missed out on the big game and the most recent school dance. *Why?* Because I didn't have control of when I could go to the bathroom. So I was stuck at home with *Planet of the Apes*. I hate that movie.

I spent that afternoon going back and forth from the couch to the toilet. My family's world went on around me. I watched as Dad and my little brother, Bobby, put the tree in the stand and set it up while Beth directed. And my mother took off to the stores with the masses to get her holiday shopping under way.

By the early evening, the tree was decorated with all but the angel on top. It was a tradition that our family gathered together around the tree and watched as one person hung the angel. It was my brother Pat's turn. He was the baby of the family. And at age nine, he was still small enough for Dad to hoist him on his shoulders. Right on cue, Bobby turned on the lights. It was a brilliant sight with all of us huddled close together.

AS THE HOLIDAY SEASON PROGRESSED, so did my illness. My nights of sleeplessness got longer, and my afternoon naps became daily. Night and day began to run together. I was beginning to fall asleep whenever I sat down for a period of time. The first time I fell asleep was in the living room rocking chair. I awoke around midnight to find my declining frame covered with a blanket. The house was silent, but my bowels were screaming.

Teachers and friends in my life were beginning to take notice of the changes to my body and in my behavior. Mr. Toms, my high school counselor, had called home to speak with my parents. He left a message on our answering machine.

"Mr. and Mrs. Street, I was calling about Junior. Several of us here at school are very concerned about him. Several teachers have commented about several changes with him over the past month and a half. I hate to be so forward, but some have mentioned that he appears to possibly be doing drugs."

My mother handled Mr. Toms and called him back shortly thereafter. I stood there listening as she spoke with him. "We don't know what is going on, Mr. Toms. We are taking him to the doctor today to try and get some answers. We will keep you informed."

The same day that Mr. Toms called was my first trip to see Dr. Levinthal to try and diagnose what was going on. When we arrived, we learned that Dr. Levinthal was still out of town and I had to see her replacement. *Great.* I was already uncomfortable and embarrassed to discuss my private bodily functions with anyone. It was compounded even more by having to talk to a new doctor.

As I walked into the patient's room, in the back of my mind, I had resigned myself to the fact that I had some sort of mortal illness that would sooner or later completely break me down.

The doctor came in, and we exchanged introductions. I cannot remember what her name was. She began by asking me several routine questions. "When did this start? How long has this been going on? Home much weight have you lost?"

I was able to answer each question easily and without hesitation. However, she finally got to a question that I felt there was a ray of hope for. She had paused from taking notes and looked me straight in the eyes and asked, "Is there any blood in your stool?"

I froze. It was the last part of the illness that I wanted to talk about. I was mortified. *What do I say? Will she think I am crazy if I tell her yes? Think.* I ran through my mind all those trips to the bathroom. Ten, fifteen, twenty times a day. Blood in the toilet, blood on the tissue, and blood in my shorts, I had to tell her. After a long pause, I spoke. "Yes." *There. I said it.* "A whole lot of blood," I added. *What a relief.*

The question opened the door to a discussion and information that I had not been prepared to volunteer. "Oh really?" She asked as she scribbled on her notepad, and then continued. "Then I presume that you have also had cramping, diarrhea, nausea."

"Yes, yes, and yes," I told her. I was starting to feel

the hope take over. I could feel myself relaxing a bit. I took a deep breath and could feel some of the burden being released as I exhaled. I crossed my fingers, hoping that she would have an answer for me. *At last, some good news perhaps?*

The exam seemed to last for an hour or so, though in reality, it was probably no more than a few minutes. She continued with scribbles on her notepad and finally said to me, "Let's go see your mother now."

We exited the office to see my mother still reading her book. I thought she looked anxious as she popped up out of her chair to greet us. She handed my mother the lab slip. "Here is a list of lab tests that Junior needs to take."

Glancing at her watch, the doctor said, "It's four right now. If you hurry, you can make it to the other side of town before five when the lab closes." She looked at my mom. "Get these labs done today. Don't wait." Then she looked at me. "Good luck, Junior. I'll call you as soon as I get the lab results." She shook our hands, and we hurried out the door.

Getting across town at that time of the afternoon was a bear. We made it though, with about five minutes to spare. I provided all of the samples: the blood, the urine, and the stool. It was a challenge to get that stool into a little cup without getting it all over myself.

The lab technician reviewed the orders one last time. "I'll get these off first thing tomorrow morning."

We thanked him and headed for home. The waiting began. It was going to be a couple of days before we heard from the doctor again. Fortunately, winter break was just days away. It was the perfect opportunity to try and take my mind off of some of my worries.

The winter break began a couple of days earlier for me than my siblings. My mother ordered me to stay home that last few days. I resisted futilely. Really, I did want to go to school. *Okay. Who am I kidding?* I was all right with staying home.

At around four that morning, there was a huge storm. That rainy and thundering night set the tone for the huge attack on my stomach. Waking up with sharp cramps, I rushed to the bathroom for what was the biggest and most painful of my bowel movements I had had to date.

About two and a half hours later, my father found me curled up with a blanket on the tile floor. I had been burning up from the stresses that had been placed on my body. Despite the outside temperature of about forty degrees, the cool tiles felt wonderful against my forehead.

My father put his arm around my waist and half-lifted, half-carried me to the couch. He handed me a pillow for my head and moved another pillow for under my knees. I tried to take deep breaths as he covered me with an old afghan.

The only thing that I thought was worse than not knowing what was wrong was sensing that my parents were helpless. My family had always been extremely fortunate with our health, and my parents had taken great pride in the fact that our family had always been self-sufficient in our abilities to tend to our needs and ailments. Aside from taking me to the doctor and seeking out medical treatment, they could only sit and watch me fall apart.

As I grew sicker, my trials would not only be a test to our family's self-sufficiency, and pride but also to our faith. My father always told us that, "No matter what happens to you, as long as you keep your faith, everything will find a way to work itself out for you." Little did I know that my faith would pay off; fate would find its way to me sooner than I could have realized.

The great part about staying home sick from school was the unusual solitude and quiet that I wasn't used to during my regular hours at home in the house. My siblings were sleeping in late, enjoying the first day of winter break. My father had run off to do some last-minute Christmas shopping, and the house was left alone to my mother and me.

My mom was milling around the kitchen and living room, shifting from one task to the next. I was in my usual post on the couch, trying to recover from the dramatic night before. I was still covered in the afghan that my father had laid over me only hours earlier.

As I was doing some channel surfing in an attempt to divert my attention from my discomfort, I felt another series of stomach cramps coming on. I tried to get comfortable, shifting from my left to my right side on the couch. In the process, I threw the blanket off of my lap. It went in one direction, and I watched as the television remote flew across the room in the other direction.

As the plastic hit the ground and made a loud snapping sound, the batteries spilled out, heading in two different directions. *Crap.* As I got up to chase after the batteries, I heard a voice from the television. "Next up. Do you have a bellyache that won't go away?" The voice was coming from Joan Lunden of *Good Morning America.* "Your stomach ailments could be more severe than you realize. We will be right back after the weather."

I stopped reaching for the batteries and waited for *Good Morning America* to resume. When it did come back, a doctor began to explain a variety of symptoms. "Abdominal pain, bleeding in your stool, weight loss, among others," he described. "If you have these symptoms, you may be in for a big surprise. You're not alone. Over one hundred thousand Americans suffer from this."

Pictures were shown of the large intestine. "Here is a healthy-looking intestine, and right next to it is the exact same shot of a diseased intestine."

This illness that the show was describing seemed to have striking similarities to what I was encountering. *These symptoms sound very similar to mine. This would be too much of a coincidence. What are the chances that I would have the same thing this doctor is describing?*

"So what is this illness?" asked Joan Lunden.

"Joan, this specifically is called Crohn's disease." When he said Crohn's disease, I felt as if a weight had been lifted off of my shoulders.

I called out across the room, "Mom, come over

here. Hurry." She made it there quickly because I had been sick. "I know some things about my illness."

"Your illness?" she asked. "What do you mean? Did the doctor call?"

I explained about the symptoms on the television show and how similar they were to my symptoms. She listened intently, and then I stated, "I think I have Crohn's disease."

CHAPTER 4

Its taste was like bad art. It cannot be described, but you know it when you see it. Absolutely offensive!

AS THE NEW YEAR BEGAN my mother and I were eager for news—any news. I tried to research Crohn's disease at the library. I wanted to know for sure what was happening to me. Once I heard about it on *Good Morning America,* I was convinced that I had Crohn's disease. I was restless. I couldn't sleep. I couldn't get comfortable on the couch. There didn't seem to be anything good on television, and I couldn't get into any book. I just couldn't concentrate. My mother and I agreed that any news, even bad news, was going to be better than no news.

Three days after the show, when the phone rang midmorning, my pulse began to race in nervous anticipation. My mother stopped ironing as we simultaneously glanced at the phone from opposite ends of the living room. Our eyes connected with each other and then went to the phone, then back to each other. I motioned for her to pick up the receiver.

She traded the iron for the phone. "Hello. Yes, he is right here. I'll have him pick up the other phone to listen in too."

I jumped from the couch and headed upstairs to the phone. I cleared my throat. "Hello, Dr. Levinthal. I'm here."

"Junior, how are you doing?" she asked.

"I'm hanging in there. Just trying to stay comfortable and not have any accidents." I had.

"Good. Good." She paused. "I got the results back for your exam, Junior—"

I interrupted. "And?" My patience was running thin.

"And," she continued, "Junior has a form of inflammatory bowel disease, Mrs. Street."

"What does that mean?" Mom asked.

"It is a form of disease with the large intestines. In some cases, it is mild. Our goal is to get Junior on medication which can send it into remission."

"And in other cases?" Mom asked.

"Well, in others," she paused, "as in Junior's case, I am afraid the patient can have extreme difficulties controlling their bowels. We need to send him to a specialist for more tests."

"More tests?" she asked. "What type of tests?"

"Mrs. Street, I don't want to get into such details over the phone. I am referring Junior to Dr. Musick, and his office will be calling you to set up an appointment. He can fill you in much more effectively and clearly with what is in store for Junior."

I thanked the doctor and hung up the phone. As I came back downstairs, I sat on the top landing, laid my head against the railing, and looked down into the living room. I could hear my mother continuing to speak with the doctor. I listened a bit more and caught my mother's half of the conversation.

I wasn't exactly sure what they were talking about, though, judging by my mother's tone of voice, she was nodding and agreeing with the doctor. At last, the phone call came to an end.

I sat on the stairs frustrated. *How long would it be before I got a call from this doctor? Would he be able to help me? Will this ever end?* I took in a deep breath and tried to hold back the tears.

I got up from the landing and headed back to the couch. The couch had become my sanctuary. It had become the place where I would stretch out, take my shoes and socks off, and try to get comfortable. My siblings were well aware that when I was lying on the couch I wasn't to be bothered. *I liked that.*

I looked at my mother, and she just smiled. "Honey, we just have to wait." She took the blanket from the back of the couch and laid it out over my bare feet. "Can I get you anything?"

"No thanks. I'll be all right," I replied. I reached out for the remote, lay out on the couch, and turned on the television to *Sports Center.* "I'm going to try to take a nap, Mom."

"Okay, sweetie."

I tried to nod off but couldn't. I was fighting too many negative thoughts. I tried to keep thinking and praying for good thoughts, but it wasn't working.

Negative ideas were seeping into my mind. I wanted to scream in anger. I tried to breathe slowly trying to control the ever growing frustration that was bubbling just below the surface. I was disappointed that I didn't get the answers that I had hoped for.

After a few minutes of slow and cleansing breaths, I was finally getting comfortable. I was starting to fade in and out of sleep as my mother moved about in the kitchen.

Then I heard my mother pick up the phone and dial. "Ginger, it's Carol." Ginger was my mother's best friend. "I just got the call from the doctor."

"No. He is asleep on the couch right now."

So she thought. I stayed motionless. I wanted to hear what she had to say to Ginger.

"Yes and no," she said. "It isn't cancer."

Cancer? The word sent chills through me.

"I know. I was relieved too."

I wasn't.

"We still have more tests to do." My mother began to choke up. "It is some sort of intestinal disease. It can be pretty serious, and the doctor hinted that Junior's case looks a little worse than others she has seen. Well, I got to run, Ginger."

I heard her set the phone down; then her footsteps grew louder as she came across the family room to check on me. I tried hard to keep my eyes closed and not give away that I was awake and had heard her half of the conversation.

She walked away once she caught a glance and went upstairs to do more chores. *Wow! They thought I had cancer.* The words had reached out to shake me.

FIVE DAYS LATER, WE WERE in Dr. Musick's office, at last hoping to get some answers. He began with the basics. He asked how I was feeling, checked my vital signs, my weight and went on and on with the questions. The repetitiveness of the questions and the check up was frustrating.

"How many bowel movements in a day? How long has this been happening? Has there been blood? How long has the bleeding been taking place?" I felt like I was in a *Peanuts* cartoon listening to the teacher; I could hear him speak, but nothing was making sense. On and on he went.

In my imagination, this visit would have been a little more simplified. I would have entered his office. He would have taken one look at my chart and said, "Junior, you are suffering from an acute case of this … *itis*. Take three pills and call me in the morning." I was naïve to think that it was going to be that simple. I didn't know a whole lot about what the doctor was talking about, but all I could say for certain was that nothing good ever had the phrase *itis* in it.

Dr. Musick began by discussing a gamut of tests that he was going to perform on me. "We'll use these tests to identify and pinpoint the severity of your illness Junior." He looked at me and stated, "I guarantee it." That line came out of his mouth just like the Men's Warehouse commercial on television. He capped it off with a confident grin.

All right, this is good. Run a few tests; skip a few days of school. I think I will be all right. My spirits began to rise. I sat up a little taller in my seat. He was giving me hope that I hadn't felt in several months. I blurted out, "When can we start?"

He laughed and said, "Slow down, Junior," as he held up his hands. "We will get to all of that."

He went into a depth of medical jargon and lost me in his sea of words. I nodded in agreement. I continued to listen and felt perplexed like Charlie Brown.

As we concluded the visit, Dr. Musick took a deep breath and said, "Junior, you're really impressive."

"Excuse me?" I asked.

"I just cannot believe what I've seen today," he replied. "From what you've told me and what I've learned about you, you've endured this for nearly three full months, lost over sixty pounds, and have only missed three days of school! It is a wonder that you have been able to walk into this office under your own power." He paused and then concluded, "Simply amazing."

THE FOLLOWING DAY, I WENT to the first of my tests alone, against my mother's protest. "It's only a test," I told her. It was nothing that she had needed to attend, "All you're going to do is sit there. It will just be a waste of your time."

In the end, she had conceded. I would have to miss first period to get this done, and I was under her strict instructions to return to school once the tests were completed.

Once I arrived for my appointment, they wasted no time.

"Just be sure to swallow the last of it down," ordered the x-ray tech. I swallowed a big gulp: *barium, how awful.*

"This will allow us a clear picture of your insides all the way down to your belly." I wasn't sure it was going to last long enough to get the pictures. With each new gulp, I could feel the barium bubble back up my throat.

"While we wait for the barium to do its job, go get undressed and meet me back out here." I followed her orders and returned immediately. I tried to get the taste out of my mouth. I felt that I had just sucked it a giant puff of dust from the chalkboard erasers. God created barium for many uses, I'm sure, but I don't think he ever meant for mankind to ingest it. Only humans would put each other through this discomfort. Its taste was like bad art, "It can't be described but you know it when you see it." *Absolutely offensive!*

WHEN THE X-RAY TECH THOUGHT everything was good, she began snapping x-ray upon x-ray. It felt like a lifetime under the x-ray techs' control. After the last picture, she excused herself and instructed me to get dressed. "When you're finished, come and see me in the office." I nodded and scooted to get out of the flimsy hospital gown; my butt was getting chilly.

I LEFT THE HOSPITAL AND went immediately to a pay phone

to give my mother a call at work. I told her that I had finished and that the tests would be back soon.

"Are you going back to class now?"

"Yeah. I'm headed back there now. I will see you after school."

About halfway between the hospital and the school, my stomach began to talk to me. *Screw this. I am going home.* Off I went. Spanish class would have to wait another day. I needed a *siesta.*

It was early afternoon, and I had about two hours to myself before the chaos in the form of my family returned. I enjoyed the quiet. It wasn't often that I was at home by myself, and as a teen, I appreciated the solitude.

I spent much of the time running what I called *the circuit:* the back and forth between the couch, the fridge, and the toilet. Though I enjoyed the quiet, I realized I was also trapped. I wanted to be outside and play tennis or take a walk, but I couldn't. I was too worried of having an accident. I wasn't sure when or where my bowels would attack me. I just knew that I couldn't take any chances.

My mother was the first one home. She came through the front door and wasted no time. "Hey, Junior. How are you doing?" There was nothing delicate about her entry ever. I was half-asleep on the couch and made little effort to answer before she asked again, "Junior, tell me what happened at the doctor's visit today."

"Terrible," I started. "It was hardly a visit. That stuff they gave me to drink only made me feel worse."

She came and sat on the couch next to me, readjusting the blanket for me in the process. "Well, do you know when they will be giving you the results?"

"I was hoping for today," I said in a disappointed tone, "but perhaps tomorrow. There was no definitive timeline."

"Well, okay then, honey." As she stood up, I heard my binder hitting the floor, spilling papers every which way. She reached down to clean it all up for me. "What is this?"

"It's my notebook, Mom." I reached out for it.

"What are all of these tally marks?" she asked.

I was a little embarrassed but said, "The tally marks are for each time I had to go to the bathroom today. I just thought it would give me something to do."

I told her that I had just finished my seventeenth trip to the john. She flipped back and couple of pages, surprised. "Wow."

"What? What?"

"That's a lot of crap."

We both laughed at her joke. Yes, it was a lot of crap.

She tossed the binder back to me and gave me a look as if she were thinking *poor thing* and headed to the kitchen. She leaned over the counter and asked me, "You want me to make you anything?"

"No. That's all right."

"Well, okay then. I'm going up the street to meet the twins at the bus." I thanked her, and I heard her slam the door *delicately* behind her as she headed off.

That night, we ate pork chops. My mother corralled the seven of us to the dinner table. This midweek family dinner was a rarity. Someone was always coming or going each weeknight. It was soccer practice one night, scouts the next, piano another evening. This made it a special occasion for the family to have a sit-down dinner together in the middle of the week.

There was little order to our dinners. We served ourselves with our first come, first serve mentality. There were rarely seconds on anything. The last person to the table often got the least. That night was different. As we loaded up our plates and began our individual feasts, my mother sat down and asked, "Who wants to say grace?"

A hush fell over the table, forks went down on the plates, and food stopped moving as we reacted to her question. *We only say grace at the holidays.* We all looked at her as if she asked us to jump off a cliff.

"Anyone?" she asked again as she glanced from one sibling to the next.

No volunteers.

My father took his seat. "Everyone, fold your hands," he commanded. "I'll start."

I sat there and closed my eyes and listened as he led us in pray. In unison, we said "amen," and we were allowed to eat.

The chatter at the table started again, but in a more solemn tone. I caught up with my siblings. My sister told me, "Señor Martin asked about you today. He hopes you get better soon." Señor was an icon at Petaluma High School. My siblings and I were part of a generation of Spanish students that sat in one of his classes.

"Well, I'll go see him when I get back," I replied.

She continued. "I will go see your other teachers tomorrow and get your make-up work."

"Thanks."

There was more small talk. The twins told me about their tales of the fourth grade. I didn't understand a word they told me. When they get excited talking, they revert back to their own language. No one in the family can understand them, except each other.

I was relieved that no one asked me about the doctor's. It was an uncomfortable subject that I wasn't prepared to explain to them. I sensed from them that they were dying to ask. I was half waiting for my brother, Bobby, to burst and just blurt out, "Junior, you just gotta tell us. Give us all of the dirty details." That didn't happen though.

After dinner, everyone went about their nightly rituals. Beth and Bobby bickered in the kitchen as they did the dishes. Bobby always accused Beth of never doing her fair share while Beth fought back by saying that Bobby never did anything right. My mother intervened a time or two only to waste breath. The bickering went on until all the dishes were done. I heard all of this from the couch as I rested and watched television.

I could hear the twins laughing and giggling as they played "Super Mario Brothers" on the Nintendo in another room. My father made the lunches as he had each night for everyone.

One by one, everyone went to bed. I decided to go to bed early.

I stood at the door and said, "Good night, everyone."

I heard many good nights in return from the different corners of the house.

As I got in bed, my mother came to tuck me in, as she had for many years as a little child. "Good night, Junior. I will see you in the morning."

"Good night, Mom." I hoped it was going to be a good night.

I stayed home from school the next day, again. I wasn't about to miss the call from the doctor's. My mother had run off in the morning to run errands: grocery shopping, paying the bills, and going to the gym. "I will be back in a few hours," I heard her say as she left.

I clutched the phone in my lap and waited. *Come on, phone. Ring.* I was getting restless. There was nothing on television. I said to myself, "This is why we go to school; because there is nothing on."

I enjoyed being home on a weekday because it was different. I looked at is as a sort of treat. I took advantage of my stay at home. I made a bowl of ice cream at nine in the morning and chased it down with an ice-cold coke. I had a feeling that it would be rough on my stomach, but I decided I would risk it. *Get wild and crazy, Junior.* My siblings would have been envious of me. No. They would have all been running to Mom, tattling on me.

In between bites and channel surfing, the phone rang. I froze each time the phone rang, afraid that the doctor was going to be the bearer of bad news. *False alarm. Stupid telemarketer!* The third time the phone rang I took a deep breath and reached for the receiver.

"Hello."

This time it was Dr. Musick.

"Junior, is that you?" the voice asked.

"Yes, it is."

"Home from school, I presume?" I heard his raspy voice say. "Are you doing okay?"

"Nothing has really changed, Doctor." I glanced over to the bowl of ice cream that I had left to melt. "I was having trouble with my bowels when I woke up this morning, so I thought it best that I stay home in case,"—a long pause before I finished in a lower voice—"you know, in case I have an accident."

"I see," he said. I could imagine him in his office that very moment thumbing his fingers through his gray beard as he contemplated what he was about to say. "Junior, I have good news and bad news. What would you like first?"

Oh, gee. Whatever should I choose? "Doctor, tell me the good news first." I needed some sort of silver lining to all the gray clouds that hovered over me at that time.

"You do not have inflammatory bowel disease."

"Really?" I was surprised. "I have to ask, though, what in the hell is inflammatory bowel disease?" I had no idea what he was talking about.

"It is a form of disease that irritates the intestines, causing bleeding and many discomforts."

"Well, I have those symptoms," I replied in bewilderment. I thought to myself, *He told me the good news first. Oh, crap.* "Wait a minute. If that is the good news, then what's the bad news?" I said, discouraged.

"You have something much worse than a simple case of IBD."

"What do I have then?"

"I don't know."

CHAPTER 5

The ordeal had left me drained,
no punned intended.

DAY TWENTY-ONE OF RAIN; day forty-two of this mysterious illness; there seemed to be no end in sight. I felt like Sally from *The Cat in the Hat,* staring outside watching the doom and gloom come down as I waited for my mother. She was taking me to my scheduled appointment for the lower GI.

We arrived at the office a whole ten minutes early. That was noteworthy in and of itself because my mother rarely arrived to any appointment on time, let alone a full ten minutes early. My siblings and I have always thought that she operates on a different clock. I could just tell that the day was going to be full of surprises. We checked in with the receptionist and sat in the waiting room. I rifled through a month-old issue of a *Sports Illustrated* while my mother paced in front of the window. The rain dripped off the gutter in the background.

A door opened from the procedure room, and a nurse stepped forward. "Junior, we're ready for you."

As I stood up, my mother came over to me and gave me a strong hug. I looked her in the eye and could see her eyes tear up.

I smiled and said, "I'll see you in a little bit, Mom." With that, I followed the nurse into the back room.

"Here is a bag to put your clothes in." She continued. "You will need to take everything off and put on this gown. When you come out, lay down on this table on your left side, like so." She demonstrated by sliding up onto the table and positioning herself on her side. She pointed me toward the bathroom so that I could change in private.

Like a poor, unsuspecting person walking on railroad tracks, I had no idea that I was about to be hit by a train. As I undressed, I thought about how cold the room was. I stood naked and held this paper-thin gown up to my torso and snickered. *This is supposed to keep me warm?*

I came out of the bathroom and sat myself up on the table. As quickly as I sat down on the table, I hopped back up. The chill of the table was too much for my bottom, so I decided to stand next to it until the technician entered.

Surprise number one. Mr. Smith came walking through the door. He was the father of a classmate of mine since the second grade.

Oh no. What if he goes home and tells Suzy about see-

ing me here? How embarrassing. I was unaware of privacy laws and confidentiality issues, so this scared the crap out of me.

Recognizing me, he smiled. "How the heck are you, Junior? It sure has been a while, hasn't it?"

"Yes, sir, Mr. Smith," I replied nervously.

"Ever since you kids left elementary school, Suzy has gotten a whole new batch of friends."

"I know. I have her in a few classes, and we talk as we pass in the halls from time to time, but that's about all."

"Oh, well." He had become engrossed in his work as we spoke. He was adjusting one knob, and then he tinkered with another set of buttons. He pointed to the table and said, "Up you go; on your left side."

I jumped right on up. As I positioned myself, I had to put my mind at ease. "Mr. Smith?"

"Yes, Junior?"

"You aren't going to tell Suzy that you saw me here, are you?"

"Not to worry. I promise." He smiled and patted me on the shoulder. He stood behind me, and as I looked up over my right shoulder, I noticed he was holding a long, cylindrical tube. He was putting something on it. "You don't want me to tell her about this part," he said as he laughed.

"This part?" I blurted out.

"Didn't anyone tell you?" He had a look of concern as he leaned over my shoulder.

"Tell me what?"

Surprise number two. "I am going to insert this tube into your rectum."

You're going to do what? What the hell? I had just been blindsided. I had never expected to have a tube shoved up my rectum. It was completely wrong, unnatural, and unfortunately, it was going to happen—right *then!* And in it went.

It was at that moment in time when I realized that the *lower GI exam sucked. It was intrusive, painful, and very unforgettable. It was a true violation of my body, mind, and soul.*

Lying on the table, I was on the verge of tears. I wanted everything to go away. I couldn't have cared less how it happened. I really truly wanted to die because of the embarrassment—just so that everything would be over with. I felt another tear roll down the side of my face.

Surprise number three.

"It will take about an hour to complete everything," Mr. Smith commented. "So just sit tight, and bear with me."

Oh, I was bearing all right. Maybe I should have paid more attention to Dr. Musick's instructions.

For the next hour, I was unbearably cold from the table and the flimsy gown that didn't do justice in covering me up. Simultaneously, my hind end was on fire. The tube that had been so gently placed in my hindquarters had a balloon attached that was used to dilate my rectum. It caused the unfathomable sensation through out the entire process of having to have a bowel movement.

Mr. Smith said, "Try to relax. It will make the process a good deal easier for you."

Easy for him to say. I stopped biting my lower lip.

The table was elevated at various angles, which put me with my head below every other part of my body.

"The idea here is that we will get the barium to travel up through the large intestines so that we can get a good picture," he said in an excited manner.

"Okay," I replied, gritting my teeth. I took a deep breath, trying to ease the tension and find a comfortable position; another deep breath. Nothing worked. I glanced at the clock to see how much longer, it felt like I had only about ten minutes to go. Unfortunately, we weren't even halfway done.

There was more movement of the table, more x-rays, more deep breaths, and more tears. I stared at the clock as the minute hand limped around. Eventually, it reached the hour mark. *Thank God.* It was almost over.

Mr. Smith informed me, "You did great." He let the table down and patted me on the shoulder. "Let me just take care of this for you." Slowly, the tube was drawn out, and I could feel the pressure being released. And with one last, swift tug, it was out. My body went limp.

He instructed me to go wash up in the bathroom. "You will be able to pass most of that barium back out right away. It can get a bit messy, but it will do you no harm."

Shaken from the ordeal, I walked gingerly to the bathroom to refresh myself.

My stomach still ached, my hind end hurt, and I

was starving since I had fasted for the past twenty-four hours.

I met my mother outside in the lobby, and she asked, "How'd it go?"

Humiliating. Painful. An absolute nightmare. "It was all right." I lied.

I don't know what my mother knew exactly about the procedure. If she did indeed know anything about it, she never seemed to let on. I wasn't going to start a conversation and fill her in on any of the details. I was sick, uncomfortable, and now completely embarrassed.

Mr. Smith had followed me out of the room and said, "Mrs. Street, your son did great."

"Thank you." She then asked, "Do you know when we will hear back?"

"We will get the films over to Dr. Musick's office ASAP. But in the meantime, it wouldn't hurt to call over to his office tomorrow to check in."

She thanked him again, and he said to me, "Good to see you again, Junior. Try to stay dry out there."

"I will," I assured him as we turned, and, together, mother and I headed home.

"Now let's go home for some rest," my mother told me. "And how about I make you a nice stack of French toast?"

"That sounds great." French toast was my favorite. Even with an unsettled stomach, I still craved a stack of her French toast.

We rode home in silence. Like the illness, the weather also seemed to have no end in sight. As I watched the rain get washed away by the wipers, I wished that I had my own wiper that could just as easily wipe away my pain too. The rain was a fitting backdrop for my situation: drab, dark, dismal.

I broke the silence near the end of the ride. "Mom, why is this happening to me?"

She didn't respond right away. I think that I blind-sided her with the question. "I don't know, honey."

"I mean, I don't think I've done anything to deserve this. Have I?"

"Of course not." She reached over and grabbed my hand. "You should ask yourself, 'Why not me?' God doesn't give people more than he thinks they can handle."

She was right. I wasn't about to let this get me down. I was determined to move forward and kick this illness.

Once we arrived home, just before we got out of the car, I made myself three solemn promises (all of which I eventually broke). One: I would never tell a soul about what happened to me that day. The social ramifications of this sort of news leaking out to my peers could be catastrophic to my image. Two: never again would any doctor, nurse, or any other person conduct such and invasive procedure of that sort on my rectum or me. I just wouldn't allow it. And three: I was going to eat the largest stack of French toast that I could imagine upon my arrival at home. At least the food would provide me some comfort from the horrors of that morning.

My mother went right to work on the French toast when we got home. I lay down on the couch and grabbed the sports page of the paper. As I skimmed the headlines, waiting patiently for breakfast, I could hear the cooking sounds coming from the kitchen: her fork hitting the side of the skillet and the sizzle as the butter landed onto the pan. My spirits were turning up. The procedure and the rain could not get me down when I had a plate full of my mother's best French toast sitting in front of me, topped off with the snowy pile of powdered sugar.

She stood over me as I took the first bite. *Mmm.* I couldn't imagine anything better tasting than that French toast at that moment.

The feast started out as a sprint and quickly turned into a walk. My stomach protested the food. I was having difficulty finishing the first piece. Sitting at the table, I tried to work on a second piece. I was failing. Suddenly, I felt as if I was socked in the gut. I looked at my plate and vomited up all of the food I had just ingested. I had broken the promise that I had made to myself. The stack of French toast would go uneaten that day.

Disappointment was rapidly becoming the norm in my life. Frustration was the main feeling. All I could hope for in those early days of this odyssey was that of a simple pleasure here or there. Anything, anything that I could sink a little hope into. There was nothing yet. *Would hope ever find me?*

THE LOWER GI TEST PROVED positive. My mother and I met with Dr. Musick three days later to get all off the details. Sitting side by side, she held my hand as he told us the news.

"Something is wrong in your belly, Junior," confirmed the good doctor. "You definitely have inflammatory bowel disease, also known as IBD. It most likely is something called ulcerative colitis. We are going to have to do another procedure to know for sure."

Oh no. Here we go again. "What else could you possibly do to me?" I gasped.

Undeterred by the interruption, he continued. "We'll be doing a colonoscopy." He pulled out a chart of the intestines. "Junior, I will be sedating you, and I will be using a camera scope to exam your intestines via your anus."

Fabulous.

"Not again," I begged, pulling away from my mother and leaning across his desk toward him. "The first time was absolutely horrific. I can't handle this again."

"Junior, we need to do this." His tone was both calm and urgent.

I glanced at both him and my mother before sitting back down to hear him out.

"We're doing this to see if there are any tumors or abscesses, and we hope that this will tell us the true extent of your illness. We can also very accurately determine the extent of your illness."

I jumped up and bumbled with the buttons as I

pulled off my shirt. "Look at me." I was using one hand to hold up my pants on my gaunt frame. "You can't sit here and tell how bad it is? Look what I've become."

My mother started to cry. At that moment, it became clear to me how fully aware my mother was of everything. *She knew.*

"I understand your frustrations, Junior." He had picked up my shirt from his desk and handed it to me. He gave me a minute to regain my composure before he continued. "I promise you that this test will get to the bottom of it."

I laughed at his joke.

As he finished explaining the procedure and its risks, I sat there resigned to the thought of another painful, invasive probe. Once again, no food for twenty-four hours and then another foreign object stuck in my rear cavity.

The next morning, I awoke at my usual time. Unlike other school days, I stood in the living room looking out the front window and waved good-bye to my four younger siblings as they paraded off to school.

My mother checked in with me as she was getting ready for work, "Junior, will you be okay today?"

"I'll be fine, Mom."

"I can get a substitute for my classes," she offered.

"Mom," I said, "you've done enough for me these past days. Besides, all I've gotta do is mix this stuff in with a little water and drink it. How hard can it be?" I said naively.

"I'll call you at lunch."

I agreed. Satisfied she gave me a hug and kiss and followed the others off to school. As she shut the door behind her, I thought once again, *How hard can this be?* I was excited. I was home alone again, I valued the peace and quiet because it was a rarity in our home with such a big family. The early morning quiet would be the silver lining of my gray day.

As per the doctor's instructions, I was to drink a laxative mixed into a gallon of water over the course of two hours. I was to be *cleansed* of all the crap from my intestines.

The medication was *rotten, rotten, rotten!* I stood over the sink and plugged my nosed as I gulped down the entire eight-ounce glass of it, nearly retching the whole time. I managed to keep the first glass down.

I turned around and went over to the stove to set the timer for fifteen minutes. I repeated the process until it was all gone. *All eight glasses.* I dreaded each gulp. I got another mouthful of water to wash the bitterness away and thought to myself, *There is no way that I can do this eight more times.*

Halfway through the medication, the bitterness of it took over. I couldn't hold down any more liquid. It was on the fourth glass or perhaps the fifth glass. I had stopped counting when I did something that I had never done before. Something that I didn't know was even physiologically possible. I took a quick swig from the glass, paused, and then began to vomit all over the sink through my nose. My stomach burned, my throat burned, and now my nostrils burned from the regurgitation.

It took me a couple of minutes to regroup. I had been taken aback from the vomiting. *Wow. No way, that just happened. I got to tell my brother Bobby when he gets home.* No sooner had I cleaned up than the phone rang.

"Hello," I answered.

"Junior, how's it going?" It was my mother.

"I am doing fine," I lied. I thought there was no need to make her worry at work. "I'm halfway through."

"Good to hear. Is there anything you want me to bring you when I come home this afternoon?" she asked.

"Not that I can think of." At that moment, something changed in my bowels. I squeezed my buttocks trying to keep everything where it should be. My bowels continued to talk to me, as did my mother.

"Okay. I will talk to you later."

"Sounds good," I quipped. "I think I hear the timer ringing. I gotta get another glass." I shifted again, standing in front of the phone.

"I love you, honey."

I rattled back, "Love you to," hung up, and sprinted to the bathroom. As I ran across the tile floor, I felt my feet slip out from under me as I tried to change direction towards the bathroom. I hit the ground hard. Surprised by the sudden fall, I hopped up and jumped down the three steps towards my destination.

I barely had time to drop my shorts before, in an uncontrollable manner that I had never experienced before, my bowels erupted. These attacks lasted for about five hours.

I never finished the last few glasses of disgust that afternoon. My mother came home to find me lying on the bathroom floor in a cold sweat. I had given up on the idea of actually leaving the bathroom, so I just stayed. It never seemed to end. When I finished one bowel movement, I just lay down and waited for the next attack.

Dr. Musick's laxative was an apparent success. I must have been purged of every impurity that my body had. My weight dropped by over ten pounds that day; most was simply water weight. The ordeal had left me drained, no punned intended. I slept straight through the night for the first time in months.

THE NEXT DAY, MY MOTHER and I left early for the hospital. It was another day of rain and pain. I thought about how much had happened to me recently—drinking the barium, the tube up me, and vomiting through my nose. *What a week.* Just thinking of those events made me nauseated. I was sick, tired, and all around crappy. As we entered the outpatient procedure area, I saw a classmate's parents seated in the waiting room. My mother went to check me in as I found a seat in the corner. I dipped my brow below a magazine in an attempt to avoid eye contact.

Right away, I heard, "Junior, what are you doing here?" It was Mr. Castro. I read the expression on his face as he gave me the once-over. It was hard to hide my frail and pale frame. He had known me for a long time and always knew me to be a husky kid.

"I'm here for a checkup." I tried to steer the conversation in another direction, so I asked, "How about you?"

It did the trick. "Oh, Jason is having the tubes in his ears replaced."

At that moment, before the conversation could go any deeper, a nurse called my name. "Junior, will you come back with me? The doctor is ready for you." *Saved by the nurse!* I said good-bye to Mr. Castro and followed the nurse behind the double doors. I glanced back and heard my mother wish me good luck. She sat down next to Mr. & Mrs. Castro. I had a sneaking suspicion at that moment that she would fill him in on the details of my ordeal.

I would later find out that she did. By the end of the week, news had traveled all over school about me—another humiliating experience for me.

It was déjà vu as I undressed and put on the hospital gown, tying it in the back. I followed a nurse to the bed, where she got me situated. She tried to start an IV. "Have you had an IV before?"

"No, I haven't," I stated. "Shouldn't you just stick the needle in and get blood?"

"Usually, that is the plan"—she felt around my forearm for a vein—"but I can't seem to find one. It's probably because you've been dehydrated from the laxatives." She stuck me again without success. I flinched in discomfort.

"How long does it take?"

"Sometimes it takes a couple of sticks," she said. "I'll give it one more time; then if that doesn't work,

I'll get another nurse to try." I winced as she stuck the needle one more. "There we go. We are in business."

"Thank goodness." I rested on my left side in the fetal position as she set up the drip line and heart monitors.

She tried to make small talk with me as she rolled me into the procedure room. "So you're a senior in high school, correct?"

"That's right."

"Did you apply to any colleges?"

"Yeah. Sonoma State University and UC Santa Cruz," I said. "I applied a couple of months ago and am just waiting to hear back."

"I loved college," she said. "You'll have a blast."

"I'm excited."

She rolled me into the procedure room and quickly reviewed the procedure. I was beginning to feel a little better because of the IV fluids, they were giving me. She finally said, "Dr. Musick is going to sedate you and you will begin to feel a bit—" The next thing I knew, I found myself in the recovery room.

That was easy. Why didn't they do that the last time? I wondered. I was greeted by Dr. Musick. "Welcome back, Junior." He smiled.

My vision and thoughts were a bit foggy, but I could begin to distinguish his silhouette and his words.

"Junior, everything is going to be fine. This gave us a clear picture of your situation. We're going to treat you and get you better starting right now." I smiled groggily and reached out for his hand.

The results of the colonoscopy proved the doctor

correct. My official diagnosis was less severe than the Crohn's disease that I had diagnosed for myself while watching *Good Morning America.* Dr. Musick told my mother and me that what I had was called ulcerative colitis. "Strictly speaking, ulcerative colitis is a chronic (ongoing) disease of the colon, or large intestine," he informed us. "You have one of the worst cases I've ever seen."

CHAPTER 6

I only wish I could have Googled it.

ONE OF MY FAVORITE MOVIES as an adult has been *The Temptations*. I've seen it four times. While I was watching it the last time, I got to thinking about the real story behind the group. So I pulled out my laptop as I have always done once a thought gets into my head, and I Googled it. Right away, the Wikipedia article about the group popped up.

I don't know where I would be today without the internet or without Wikipedia. It has become my lifeline for the quick fix when I am in need of a answer to a question that has popped into my head. It's always been my nature to learn more and search for answers when I've got questions. Perhaps it's because I've got an innate curiosity; perhaps it's because I've been a lifelong student or because I am a teacher.

When I look back on my senior year of high school, I recall how I'd done very much the same thing once I was diagnosed with ulcerative colitis. I only wish I could have Googled it.

I committed myself to learn all that I could about the disease. I thought that by understanding colitis that it would only help to empower me. Ulcerative colitis is a form of inflammatory bowel disease (IBD). I learned that thousands of individuals are diagnosed with it each year. And that on the spectrum of intestinal disorders, the mildest of cases are called inflammatory bowel syndrome, IBD, then colitis, and the worst of it all, is Crohn's disease.

"IBS should never be mistaken for IBD, colitis or Crohn's," a doctor once told me. IBS has often been referred to as a spastic colon, which occurs when the muscles contract. There is no actual intestinal inflammation caused by IBS.

IBD, on the other hand, does have inflammation and is categorized as one of two illnesses: colitis or Crohn's. In the simplest of explanations that I have researched, colitis is a chronic, ongoing disease of the colon. It is a superficial illness within the colon that is evident by the inflammation and ulcers of the colon's surface (colon mucosa), the inner lining of the intestines. The inflammation was the cause of my uncontrollable bowels, the bleeding, the diarrhea, the cramping, and the weight loss.

All of this information that I gathered helped prepare me to answer the throngs of questions that I was expecting to receive when I arrived back at school after my three-day absence.

PRIOR TO MY DIAGNOSIS, I had not missed a day of senior year. In fact, I hadn't missed a day of school since the first grade. It had been my goal to have perfect attendance through high school. Those plans had gotten derailed drastically with the onset of the illness. I was disappointed that I wouldn't be able to lay claim to perfect attendance, but I got over that quickly. There were more important things in life, like my health.

The fact that I had been in and out of class for the past couple of months was a red flag to many of my close friends. When I finally arrived back at school, I was greeted with many curious looks and a lot of questions by friends, classmates, and teachers. Everyone wanted to know something, and the teachers just wanted to check in. I think it was intriguing for my peers to learn why I had been away.

"Hey, Junior. Where've you been?" shouted out one classmate.

"I've been around," I quipped, hoping that I would be able to pass it off and move on. "I had a bad case of the flu."

"Oh," he said. I couldn't look at him. I was very self-conscious knowing that he was staring at me. As I went from class to class, I repeated similar conversations with other classmates, friends, and teachers. It started to get easier as I relayed the story over and over.

I headed off a few rumors, and I fueled a few others just for kicks and giggles.

At break between classes, Jason, the classmate who was at the hospital, said, "My Dad said that you had cancer. It isn't true, is it?" Jason was never one for subtlety, and I noticed that several other sets of ears were leaning in to hear my answer.

I shook my head, "Fortunately no, but the doctors did think that they were going to have to send me away to a sanitarium for a year." They gasped. "Kind of like Doc Holiday in the movie *Tombstone.*"

"Really?"

"Oh yeah. It was a real possibility."

"Wow," he said, stunned. "So what was wrong then?"

Since I was starting to feel a bit more comfortable sharing my woes I threw caution to the wind and figured what the hell, so I told him and the rest of my peers surrounding me at that moment, "I have something called ulcerative colitis."

By their responses, not many of them knew what it was. Most of them were probably very much like myself and had never even heard of it.

I explained to what colitis was all about; the ulcers, the weight loss, and the fatigue, choosing to omit the more personal details about the bowel movements, blood, diarrhea, and accidents.

The news of my illness spread throughout the school community and our town. It seemed that everyone had a friend or a friend of a friend who was also suffering of colitis. It gave me a little bit of comfort knowing that I was not alone.

I learned from my doctor that every case of colitis is different and unique. I have likened it in many regards to diabetes. Neither disease is curable, though they can both be very manageable with proper care and diet.

The management of each case varies greatly. In some cases, people have had bouts with it once or twice and take minimal amounts of medication while some have learned how to control it and never had any real serious issues from the illness.

In my case, as with so many other people, obtaining equilibrium of my body had proven difficult and seemed doubtful. I had extreme difficulties trying to control the illness. My greatest fear was that I was going to end up housebound. I envisioned the real possibility that I wasn't going to be able to ever leave my house due to my inability to control my bowels. Tennis, school, and life in general would have to take a backseat to my bowels, permanently.

WITH THE DIAGNOSIS CONFIRMED BY the colonoscopy, Dr. Musick immediately put me on two medications: Asacol and a steroid called Prednisone. My body slowly responded to the medications over the remaining four months of my senior year.

My recovery was a difficult process. The medications helped get me into a stage of remission, but it was a tenuous situation at best. Each time I saw signs of improvement, I seemed to have an attack and regress. I felt as if I was taking three steps forward and two steps back.

I first started to notice improvement and control over my bowels about a week after I began the medications. I was making fewer trips to the bathroom. My tally sheet was getting down to about ten trips a day. And I no longer felt the sudden urges that had come to be the norm and scare the hell out of me. The bleeding began to stop also.

Through the spring semester, I was continuing to show the mixed signs of recovery. My stomach still ached much of the time but with less intensity and for shorter periods of time. I would find myself relaxed in class, feeling calm, and then I felt as if someone had given me a swift hit to the gut. I would hunch over in my desk, hoping no one would notice. My teachers had all agreed to help me when I was having troubles. I had a free and unlimited bathroom pass that I could use when the situation warranted it. As a teacher myself, I understand and appreciate their help. It wasn't just a show of altruism on their part. None of them were interested seeing me have an accident in the middle of their classroom.

At one of my follow-up appointments, I stepped on the scale and saw that I had gained back about twenty of the nearly sixty pounds that I had lost.

"Things are looking good, Junior," said Dr. Musick as he reviewed my charts. "How've you been feeling?"

"Actually, a little better each day."

"Good to hear." He scribbled notes down on his paper. "I think that the medications that I have you on will be the proper protocol for a while."

I nodded, and he continued.

"I am encouraged that by the way you are responding to the meds so far. You will make a full recovery."

I couldn't help but smile. "Great."

"There is one other medication I need you to take."

"What is it?"

"Your blood counts have been extremely low, and you are anemic."

"I am?" I asked. "What does that mean?"

"Well, let me ask you. Are you tired? Feel fatigued? Always seem to be rundown?"

I thought about it for a second. "Yes. Even though I've been starting to feel stronger, I've always seem to be tired."

"That is what I suspected," he confirmed. "Here is a prescription for iron pills." I thanked him, and then he said, "Do you have any other questions?"

"None that I can think of right now," I said. I shook his hand and went on my way. I was told to be in touch and to call if I needed anything. Otherwise, Dr. Musick told me to come back in a month.

I felt some reserved optimism. I wanted to be positive but was guarded about being too upbeat.

The iron pills were to supplement my body's natural production of red blood cells. The excessive bleeding throughout the illness had depleted my red blood cell count, which was the cause of my anemia. As Dr. Musick had explained to me the anemia had left me with fatigue; weakness; abdominal pain; and, from time to time, dizziness.

I tried hard to swallow the pills whole, but the iron was too strong for my sensitive belly. No sooner would it hit my belly than I would be hanging over the toilet, vomiting it back up.

The next day, I repeated the process. I popped the pill and then vomited it back into the toilet. No one ever accused me of not being persistent; I tried for a third day. No success. Again, I vomited. As I sat by the toilet, I recalled what my father told me on many occasions. "There is more than one way to solve a problem, Junior."

His words rang true. The next attempt, I took the pill and cut it in half and swallowed. Nothing happened—not right away. It took about thirty minutes before I found myself again with my head in the toilet. *Cut it in quarters.* I divided the pill into four pieces and wrapped them in a piece of toast. It worked. *Thanks dad!*

Success at last! Four times a day, I repeated the process. Within a week, I was holding my head up high and wasn't holding my stomach anymore.

As my red blood count increased, so did my energy levels. I was back on the tennis courts for the high school varsity tennis team. It was exciting.

As graduation day approached, I had reason to celebrate. I had regained some of the color in my complexion, along with about half of the weight that I had lost too. I felt good, healthy, and happy. Most importantly, my bowels were under control, and I was only having four to five movements a day. There were no urgent trips to the bathroom, no blood and most importantly no accidents. Graduation day was great. I was ready to take my plunge into the great, wide world beyond the walls of Petaluma High School. I was stronger and healthier, and fit to conquer the world.

CHAPTER 7

Patience is a virtue

COLITIS TAUGHT ME THAT LIFE isn't always fair. It was the most valuable lesson that I learned my senior year in high school.

So full of questions yet so empty without answers.

Why?—I was young and suppose to be healthy.

Why me?—Didn't I take care of my body? I thought I had.

Why did I get this?—Perhaps it was my genetics; at least I could have blamed my parents then.

Why did God make me suffer?—I'd played by all of the rules. I worked hard. I exercised daily, and I was good citizen. If there was ever a person who didn't deserve this, it was me. I wasn't about to feel sorry for myself; that was one lesson my parents taught me.

I didn't want to let this get me down. I wanted

to start my life after high school with hope and optimism. My two goals after high school were to play college tennis and to earn a degree in history. I had a passion for both, and they were well within my grasp. All I had to do was reach out and grab them.

I spent the next two years at a local community college, balancing my time between studies and three hours of daily tennis practice. My coach, Izzy Derkos, was a former football coach and a fanatic for conditioning whipping us into shape.

Each practice began with coach's misleading statement, "We're going to start with a little *mini conditioning.*" There was no such thing as mini conditioning. Some days we did ten minutes of speed work. Others days we trained for more than an hour; it was just what I needed. Each day I felt stronger and more energized. Coach showed me how to work harder than I had ever worked before. By the end of my first season on the team, I was in the best physical shape of my life.

MY ILLNESS WAS SPORADIC DURING the two years of junior college. I battled for control on and off the tennis court. I tried to keep the matter private. Only Coach and my best friend, Ross, were aware of the full extent of my situation.

As my strength and condition improved, many of my symptoms did indeed go away. There would be months when I would go without incident, and then there were periods of time when I would have uncontrollable bouts of diarrhea, cramps, and bleeding.

I never knew when or where an attack would happen to me, so I prepared myself for the worst at all times. I made it a point to always know where the closest bathroom was at all times. I carried an extra change of clothing. These are simple actions that I still practice today to control any potential messes.

By the end of junior college, I had gotten a pretty good handle on my situation. Accidents happened, but they were becoming less frequent. I tried to shrug them off as no big deal, but I couldn't. I remember lying in bed one night thinking about an accident from earlier that day. I cried myself to sleep as I begged God to help me. I waited, but I heard nothing but silence. I resigned myself that this was out of my control and just the way my life was going to be.

AFTER COMMUNITY COLLEGE, I WAS comfortable enough in my control of my body and the timing just seemed right to fulfill my dream of attending a four-year school and playing collegiate tennis.

Tennis was all I thought about. As I lay in bed nearly every night, I imagined that I was playing the most important match of my life—the match for a national championship. It was just as exciting the hundredth time I dreamed of it as it was the first time.

Even though I was thrilled to be away from home at a four-year college, the new surroundings were difficult. Since I'd never been an outgoing person, I struggled adjusting to roommates, classmates, and teammates. I was immediately homesick, and I tried to cope by throwing myself one hundred percent into my studies and tennis.

I missed my girlfriend, Tiffany—my first love. I asked myself repeatedly, *Why am I here? Why did I leave her?*

My stomach began to really flare up as a result of the stress. The cramping, the bleeding, and the uncontrollable bowels all returned.

My saving grace was Prednisone, a steroid that increases hormones used to suppress inflammation in the body. In my case, the medication was being used to keep my stomach from bleeding and attempt to control my bowel movements.

Prednisone had worked well while I was in community college but then began losing its effect. My doctor prescribed a specific dose, but I started to use the medication more often and on an as-needed basis. When I had an attack, I popped some extra prednisone. It helped.

While the drug helped to maintain a fragile control over my bowels, it was quickly taking control of me.

I also tried to cope with alcohol, courtesy of my teammates. I'd never drank before, but it seemed to help me cope with all of my loneliness. It flushed away my emotional pain and continued to burn up my delicate insides, so I took more pills.

As the cycle perpetuated, I was becoming a victim to the terrible side effects. I was nervous, hyperactive, and struggled to pay attention in class. One day after class my anatomy professor asked, "Junior, are you okay?"

"What? Why do you ask?"

"You just seem anxious."

"No, I'm fine," I said, shaking my left foot up and down as I sat at my desk trying to hide my situation.

The excessive hormones produced by the drug were taking a toll on my emotions. The stress created from being away from home and my girlfriend, only added to my struggles. I became increasingly reclusive and short-tempered. I was absolutely miserable with everything.

I struggled at practice and my game suffered. Tennis is a very cerebral game. My focus on the tennis court diminished. I frequently threw my racquet in frustration, and when that didn't satisfy me, I would shout an expletive, which was completely out of character for me and unacceptable tennis conduct.

On our last day of fall practice a teammate, Tim questioned a line-call of mine. "Are you sure that ball was out?"

"Yeah, I saw it out," I replied.

"You have to be kidding me," as he ran to my side of the court to look for a ball mark.

Usually I wasn't fazed by an opponent questioning a call. It was part of the game, but that day was different. I raised my racquet and felt the rage take hold in my hands. I took a deep breath, backed away from him, and threw my racquet up against the fence. The other players stopped dead on their courts. I glanced around as I went to grab my racquet. I looked back at

Tim, "You win. I quit. I'm not going to waste my time arguing with you about a stupid line call."

Coach rushed over from three courts away. "What the hell is the problem here?" he demanded. I stood there silently. He grabbed me by the arm, pulling me towards him. "I'm tired of this crap, Junior. You've been causing me nothing but headaches. I don't know why I even bothered bringing you here."

I jerked my arm away and pulled back from him. We were surrounded by the entire team. "I need to cool off. I'll see you tomorrow."

"Not so fast, Junior," he raised his voice. "You threw your racquet; you know what the penalty is for that." I knew all too well, thirty push-ups. "Everyone, gather around and let's count for Junior."

I got down on my hands and knees and began, "One, two, three ..." The count went on. Around number twenty-five, I had nothing left and collapsed on the court, tired, cold, and outright miserable. He got down on the ground next to me, screaming in my ear, "Finish these, Junior. You're just a waste of talent."

I started to cry uncontrollably. Tim began to laugh, "Look everyone. Junior is crying like a little baby." I stood up and tried to collect myself, wiping away the tears with the back of my hand. I watched as Tim walked over and picked up my racquet and threw it two courts down.

"Practice is over," Coach declared. "Get out of here, Junior." I looked around at my teammates. The other players looked away as an awkward silence surrounded us all.

As Coach walked away, I rushed towards Tim, jumping on his back and knocking him down to the ground. As we grappled back and forth, we pushed and shoved each other until I managed to gain the upper hand. Then I began to strangle him. I had both hands fully wrapped around his neck. As I squeezed my hands harder and harder around his neck, I watched in slow motion as he gasped for air.

As the team broke us apart, I wiped my lip and saw blood. I'd crossed the line. I headed away for my gear. Tim came after me, grabbing the back of my shirt and pulling me back towards him. I spun around towards him, throwing several punches. The team frantically pulled us away from each other as he landed one good punch across my jaw. Once we were finally broken apart for good, I grabbed my tennis bag, got to my bike, and headed off into the depths of the campus.

As I rode away, my rage subsided. I needed a place to hide. I snuck into one of the dorms and found a corner and hid under the stairwell all night. I cried as I realized my collegiate tennis dreams were gone. I could hear people running up and down the stairwell. The fight seemed to be the latest buzz around school.

The temperature dipped to sub-freezing that night, but the building was heated. I snuck into the community showers of one of the dorms to get cleaned up. I was scared, angry, and sick.

Early the next morning, I quietly went back to my apartment, careful not to let anyone see me. I packed up what I could of my clothes and tennis equipment. Leaving everything else behind, I wrote a terse note to the landlord with one more check and then headed to the airport. I didn't even take my finals. I just left.

I didn't say goodbye to my roommates. I didn't say goodbye to my teammates, and I didn't say goodbye to Coach. All I said goodbye to on that frigid December morning were my dreams.

I arrived home that evening to my waiting parents. They had received a call earlier that morning by Coach, who had told them that I was missing. They opened the door and opened their arms to me. They embraced me as I had hoped that they would. No one said a word. We just held each other. My crying said it all.

For the first and only time in my life, I thought of suicide.

CHAPTER 8

*Crack my belly open and take
out all of the bad parts.*

SOMETHING NEEDED TO CHANGE. LIKE a broken clock, I had stopped ticking, and I needed fixing. I thought of the fabled story my father used to read to me about the king's men. I wasn't sure that anyone would be able to put me back together again. The holiday season didn't seem so merry to me. I spent the holidays with my family in quiet solitude. I didn't speak much to anyone. I didn't return phone calls to friends or family; it was looking to be a winter of discontent. I was ashamed and embarrassed, so I kept to myself. Most days I sprawled out on the couch or on my bed reading Tom Clancy, John Grisham, Nelson DeMille, and a hodgepodge of others that were going to keep me occupied throughout the holiday season. The great thing about the books, I figured, was that I could set my book down when I had an attack and easily return to it after.

As Christmas approached, my parents wanted a fresh start. "Sometimes it's just best to start over," my father told me. "Your mother and I want a fresh start for you." *Start over.* My father, a man of few words, always spoke powerfully. He was right; let's start over.

MY PARENTS AND I MET with my new doctor three days before the New Year. I had resigned myself to feeling that I was stuck in a perpetual downward cycle of misery. Enter my new doctor, Dr. Myers. As we exchanged handshakes and introductions, I sensed that something was about to change.

Dr. Myers stood eye to eye with me in a white lab coat and a matching head of white hair. He began, "Junior, colitis is a disease that, just thirty years ago, was thought to be nearly insurmountable. You look like you have had a rough stretch in the past few years." He glanced at the three of us and continued, "I want you to know that I've reviewed your case, and I won't kid around, it is pretty severe. But that's all right. I'm going to show you and your parents," he said, using his pen he pointed to each of us individually, "how we're going to manage this. It is very treatable."

Both my mother and father put their arms around me, as they were reassured by my new doctor. Unlike my previous doctor, he was in no hurry to prescribe medications. "I don't want to mask any problems with meds," he spoke with refreshing confidence. "We will get you fixed up right away though."

"How bad is it?" I asked.

"Terrible," he said, "usually someone suffering from colitis has an area of irritation that stretches typically 10 to 20 percent of the large intestines. You, on the other hand, have nearly your entire large intestine bleeding."

He pointed to his chart of the large intestine as we spoke. "Do you have any questions before I continue?"

"How long will this whole process take?" I asked, "I accepted the fact that I am never going to have a normal life."

Dr. Myers reacted strongly to the notion, "You are absolutely wrong, Junior. You can have a normal healthy life. It may take a while, and it will require some hard work and patience, but it can be done. You just have to trust me."

"Mr. and Mrs. Street, the medications haven't been working, and I am strongly recommending surgery for Junior."

I started to cry. It wasn't quite what I expected. "Surgery?" My mother asked. "Are you sure that it's necessary?"

"Yes," he said, "Junior is a strong young man but because of the colitis he's been unable to live the quality of life that he deserves to live."

"But he is only twenty," she exclaimed. I sat quietly wiping a tear away as I watched the verbal exchange back and forth.

"I realize that," he leaned forward in his chair, "but

many patients with colitis end up having surgery of one degree or another in their lifetime."

I looked at my mother. "Mom, we need to get all the information that we can."

She took a deep breath, "I know, I know." Reaching out, she held my hand.

AT DR. MYER'S RECOMMENDATION, I met with the surgeon, Dr. James Stricker. I went with Tiffany for the consult. He was a small man in stature. At six foot one inches, I towered over his tiny frame of about five foot five inches. I would have described him as a rather typically bookish doctor. After exchanging pleasantries with Tiffany and me, he wasted no time getting down to business.

"I reviewed your files and Dr. Myer's notes," he began. "I wanted you to know that I have worked with Dr. Myers for many years, and he has only referred his patients to me when he doesn't see any other alternatives."

I gave him a nod of understanding.

"He noted in the file that you are one of the most severe cases that he has ever seen." He hesitated, looking me in the eye, and continued, "And after reviewing your chart, I would have to agree with him."

I was speechless. I didn't feel much reason for hope at that point. He had instantly convinced me that this was the right decision to make. I asked, "So, at this time, with all of the data in front of you, do you believe that this surgery is the best medical option for me?"

"Absolutely." He didn't flinch.

The surgery that he was discussing with me was a total colectomy. This would involve the complete removal of my large intestine; in lieu of a large intestine, a pouch would be formed out of the small intestine. This pouch would serve in place of the large intestine as a reservoir for the waste prior to bowel movements. It was simple enough on paper. Of course, there were complications.

In most cases, it would require multiple surgeries. The first surgery would be done to remove the intestines and create the pouch. In order to allow the stitches to heal, a stoma would be created in the abdomen. The stoma would connect to an ostomy bag, in which I would essentially poop out my stomach. The bag would hold the feces until I was ready to dump it. This was done in order to allow time for the pouch to heal properly and to prevent possible bacterial infections.

The hopeful fire that Dr. Myers lit in me had been stoked by Dr. Stricker's words. I got a positive vibe from him in that visit. Dr. Stricker was a good man.

He pulled out a chart of the intestines to explain the procedure. "I will make a ten-inch cut down your abdomen about here."

As he spoke, I began to imagine myself without colitis. *Oh to be healthy,* I yearned. That was a world that had seemed long forgotten. It was difficult to grasp the concept of feeling and being healthy because it had been such a long time since I had actually been healthy. I had often asked myself, *What is it like to feel normal?* What a loaded question.

I was brought back to the doctor with a gentle

nudge by Tiffany. "What did you ask?" I looked up at him and Tiffany. "I was drifting a little. My stomach is getting a little uptight." I lied.

"What do you think of what I've told you, Junior?" he asked.

"I am ready." I was eager to do it. "Let's do it."

I was convinced. I thought to myself, *Crack my belly open and take out all of the bad parts.*

THE SURGERY WAS TO TAKE place on March 13th—a Friday. With all of the superstition around the date, friends, and family members thought I was crazy. Leading up to the surgery, several friends and family members asked, "Aren't you worried about having a bad luck day?"

I replied, "I just hope the surgeon doesn't have a bad day."

I didn't take much stock in the superstition myself. *It's just a day.* I could hear my father saying, "How many times have I told you, you make your own luck, Junior." Yes, you do!

SURGERY WAS A SUCCESS. THE colitis was gone. Dr. Stricker informed my parents in the waiting room, "Junior is now officially on his way to a full recovery." I took a big sigh of relief. "No more colitis," Dr. Stricker assured me.

While the pain from the incisions was intense, my body felt better from head to toe. Within days following the surgery, my belly didn't ache any more. It was great to be able to go through a day without the threat or urge of having to suddenly use a bathroom.

After being stuck and poked with needles for a week, my tolerance for nurses and doctors was running out. The morphine, the hospital food, and the catheter were terrible. I was ready to go home.

As I awoke the last morning in the hospital, I was renewed with excitement. I knew that the tubes were going to be removed, and I could return home to finish my recovery. For the first time in this three-year ordeal with colitis, I was starting to feel healthy. I hadn't felt this way in several years. I had a healthy life ahead of me. And I was looking forward to playing tennis again someday soon.

CHAPTER 9

*Just because things didn't work out
the way you planned them doesn't
mean they didn't work out well.*

—Unknown

WHEN I LEFT THE HOSPITAL eleven years ago, my doctor had told me to go home and live a long healthy life. The surgery had cured me of my colitis. That was short lived; it lasted five days.

After my release from the hospital, I returned for my first follow up consultation with my surgeon, Dr. Stricker. My parents and I met with him in his San Francisco office.

"Good morning everyone," he began, "How are you feeling today, Junior?" I sat on the exam table as he inspected the incision on my belly.

"I'm doing well," I told him, "the incision is uncomfortable, but it seems to be healing nicely."

"Are you following the protocol we gave you to clean and tend to it?"

"Yep," I assured him, "My mother or father helps me every day." I smiled as I gestured towards them.

"Excellent," he said, flipping through some papers, "this visit is to see how you are progressing and to fill you in on some changes to expect in your life."

"Okay," I nodded, "sure thing."

"There are some lifestyle changes that you are going to have to adapt to," he paused. "But I wanted to go over a more pressing issue with you and your family first."

When he said *pressing*, I felt an alarm go off in my mind. There was a huge lump in my throat, and my heart began to race. I reached out to grab my father's hand. I shifted to try and find a more comfortable position to relieve the pain from the twelve-inch-long vertical incision in my belly. "What is it that we need to talk about?"

He thumbed through the notes in front of him, "Well, we've received the pathology reports back from our lab in Oakland. And I wanted to take a few moments to go over the results with you."

He took in a deep breath. He made eye contact with each of the three of us before he continued. "The lab report shows that the colon was indeed in a terrible shape. As everyone has said before, Junior, it was as bad as any one had ever seen."

That got a smile and laugh out of me. "Do I get some sort of award for that?"

He shook his head. "I wish there was one, but I have some unfortunate news too." My mother's eyes flared and my father sat up in his chair. "The pathology results show that this was not ulcerative colitis as we had all reported." He made eye contact with my mother, my mother, and myself. "It's Crohn's disease."

That was rather unexpected.

"So what does that mean for me then?"

"Contrary to what we had expected, this surgery will not cure the Crohn's disease." He was cool and methodical. "You see, in a small fraction of cases, the two are indistinctive."

"What does this all mean?" My mother demanded. "How could this be?"

"Well allow me to explain. Colitis is a superficial irritation of the intestines, while Crohn's can go deeper into the surface and into other parts of the GI tract."

My mother continued her verbal offensive. "So you're saying that this was an unnecessary surgery?" I could see the rage in her body as her eyes narrowed.

"Oh no, not at all," he said. My mother looked like she was about to go ballistic. I couldn't take it. I slid back on the table, trying to inch away from her. I was more afraid of her reaction than the disease at that moment.

"In many cases, the only way to really determine the true identity of the illness is to actually go in and remove a piece of the inflamed intestines and perform a biopsy. That is precisely what we did with, Junior."

"You didn't perform just a biopsy," my mother shouted. "You took out his entire large intestine."

"I'm going to be frank with you, Mrs. Street. I understand your frustrations. However, your son needed this operation. We took out all of the damaged intestines. This surgery will give him the opportunity of living a healthy life; a life that we have all wanted for him."

He turned towards me and continued, "Junior, there is no way of knowing whether or not you will ever have another flare up or not. Statistically speaking, if it does re-emerge it won't be for five to seven years."

I slouched lower in my seat, and shifted in agony. "Can I be healthy now since I've had this surgery?"

"Absolutely," he declared. We talked for a few more minutes about treatment plans, proper nutrition, and healthy lifestyle suggestions.

When we finished he stood up and exchanged handshakes with us all. "I'll want to see you in a couple of weeks to examine that incision and follow up."

"Is there anything else that we should do since this is not what we expected?" I asked.

"Not at the moment," he replied. "I'll be in contact with Dr. Myers, and he will check in with you every few months. If you notice any of your symptoms coming back, contact him immediately. Is that understood?"

I nodded in agreement.

The doctor excused himself, and I sat quietly with my parents in the exam room.

I tried to speak, but nothing came out. I had lost my voice. My mother just cried. My father broke the silence, "Let's go. I know it wasn't what we were expecting or hoping for. But we will make it work."

He helped me off the exam table, "Just because things don't work out the way you expected, doesn't mean that they can't work out well."

My mother wiped away the tears. "This wasn't the way it was supposed to be though." My father reached out for her hand.

"Let's get out of here," he said and led the way out of the exam room.

IN THE YEARS SINCE MY surgery, I have never taken a day for granted. I've tried to live my life fully and not let the Crohn's keep me from a challenge. I've done numerous activities that many people might not have said were possible because of my Crohn's, like running 199 mile relay race in twenty-four hours, completing three marathons, and competing in triathlons; each time purposely pushing the limits of my body and mind.

My older brother, Steve, likes to tease me about my activities, "Why do you do this Junior? Running's for the birds."

The only answer I've ever given him is, "Because I can."

CHAPTER 10

A day that will live in infamy…

–Franklin D. Roosevelt

THE SURGERY HAD PROVED TO be my ticket back to health. It had been a little over two years since the colonectomy, and for me, graduation marked the end of a tumultuous college career.

I had re-enrolled in college six months after surgery and dove headfirst into my studies. I chose to pursue my passions and major in history. Sonoma State was appealing because it was local. It was seven miles from my parents' home. I had no interest in being on my own again, and Sonoma State offered me a means to an end.

I even managed to get back on the courts and play a few matches on the men's tennis team. It wasn't the spectacular tennis that I had spent nights dreaming about, but I did achieve a goal: I competed and played Division II tennis. I was on the courts, back in my comfort zone.

GRADUATING FROM COLLEGE WAS THE biggest accomplishment of my life at that point. I was proud of myself and relieved. I celebrated with my family and friends that afternoon with everyone who had supported me in my struggles and my journeys. I had had my doubts that this day would ever come. Thank goodness I made it.

I went on with my life enrolling in the teaching credential program at Chapman University where I earned both an elementary teaching credential and a secondary teaching credential.

AS I APPROACHED THE TAIL end of the teaching program, I began to experience stomach discomfort and cramps again. I remembering being in the middle of a class when I was student teaching, and I had to rush to the bathroom; just like the old days. *Oh, that doesn't feel good.*

I was able to finish the class, then I hustled out again to find a bathroom. That afternoon, I headed back home, and I lay down on the couch to take a rest. At one point early in the evening, I suddenly had the huge urge to go to the bathroom. It was a feeling that I hadn't felt in over three years.

I was dismayed. Dr. Stricker had assured me that I'd have at least three to five good years before symptoms of the Crohn's would resurface. That evening, I looked at a calendar in my room. *I guess my time is up.* He was right. Almost three years to the day. The surgery had given me a large chunk of my life back—for a little while.

In the coming weeks, all of the symptoms began to come back. I noticed blood again in my stool. It was a telltale signal that my illness was beginning to rear its ugly head again.

I was devastated. *Just when I was thinking that everything in my life was finally going my way. Not now. Not ever again.*

No sooner were some of the symptoms beginning to re-emerge than I went in for an annual check-up with my family practitioner.

I met with my doctor and the first words out of his mouth was, "Junior, you look a little pale," he opened my file. "I see that you have Crohn's disease. Are you feeling all right?"

"I've been starting to show some symptoms again," I replied.

"Well, we better run some blood tests." He handed me a lab order, "and I'll get in touch with Dr. Myers for you."

Reluctantly, I went downstairs to give blood. He also had scheduled me for an appointment with Dr. Myers for a colonoscopy. *Another anal probe, great.* They are going to look up my posterior again. I went and completed my blood tests and then waited.

THE PHONE CALL CAME A week later. "Junior, this is Dr. Myers. We need to talk." The pit of my stomach began to turn. I intuitively knew what was coming next. "The test results show that the Crohn's has returned." He paused while I took in a deep breath. "It is worse than before. Your blood counts are also deficient. You are anemic and susceptible to illnesses."

"So where do we go from here?" I asked very coldly.

"We get you on a few good drugs," he declared. "I will not put you back on Prednisone. Lord knows how that affected you before. These alternative medications are good. You will get stronger again."

DR. MYERS PUT ME ON old Crohn's drug called Asacol and Imuran. The combination of the two was going to combat the inflammation and keep it from spreading throughout the bowels. *What were a few more drugs in my system going to do anyways?* I had assured myself.

The next morning, I awoke with a renewed intensity in my stomach. It was a familiar burn, the type of burn that you only get when something is seriously wrong. I knew at that moment that the Crohn's was really back.

I wanted to believe that the entire illness was in my mind. I wished that I hadn't gone to the doctors and that I hadn't been tested. I tried to wish it all away. After all, it was the doctor who had told me I was sick. Dr. Myers told me, "The numbers don't lie, Junior. Your Crohn's is active again."

The drugs didn't help. Within a month, I was in great distress. Every bowel movement was full of blood. The more I bled, the more anemic I got. People began to ask my parents questions, "Is Junior sick again?"

"Of course not," My mother would respond. "Why do you ask?"

"He looks so pale. Look at his jaw line, how gaunt he looks."

When those comments got back to me later, I took a long look in the mirror. I studied my jaw line and took off my shirt to look at my side profile. Then I noticed it: my ribs. I had always been a husky individual. I never could see my ribs.

In a panic, I stepped in the scale. I hadn't weighed myself in some time, but I did know that I was around one hundred eighty pounds. The scale wouldn't lie to me. *Would it?*

"One seventy?" I began to panic. *Ten pounds?* It wasn't possible. I was eating well. I wasn't having too many stomachaches. Yes, my bowel movements were increasing and my weight was decreasing. The slide that had begun slowly in March of 2001 began to snowball through December 2001.

Before I knew it, I was a paltry 140 pounds.

I RETURNED TO SEE DR. Myers in early December. I needed help, and he was the only one that I trusted. I hadn't realized it at the time, though in hindsight, I realized how close I was to being incapacitated. I was headed toward a situation that would leave me stuck at home. Nearly fully disabled (by the letter of the law), I was nearly housebound.

I was never one for too many doctor's visit. Very much to the same line of thinking as my mother, I just wanted to let the illness run its course and it would fade away. What I didn't understand or appreciate at that time was the fact that Crohn's was not just an illness.

This wasn't the flu, a simple bellyache, or a stomach virus. It was a major medical malady. If I wasn't treated accordingly, not only would I be stricken down continually, I could very well indeed die.

"Junior," Dr. Myers announced, "I want to run a few more tests. I need to see you in my office this week."

"Sure thing," I agreed. I was hesitant about getting more tests, but I went to get the tests completed with guarded optimism. The tests were needed for him to get to the bottom of this (no pun intended).

What were my other medical options? I did not see a whole realm of positive thoughts. *More surgery? An Ostomy bag?* Neither of these were appealing alternatives. I was tempted and willing to sell my soul to the devil for an end to all of my misery.

That night, amid an upset stomach and multiple bowel movements, I began to imagine myself beginning to feel better. I walked through my upcoming appointment with Dr. Myer's in my mind. I walked into the room, and he said, "I have the cure for you, Junior." In his hand was the holy grail for the illness. "This shot will end your nightmare." Once I received the shot, I would be returned to my good health, never knowing how sick I had ever been.

The dream, though, was interrupted by an accident in my shorts. It was two in the morning, and I was taking a shower, getting cleaned up, and then changed the sheets. The old sheets were again buried deep in the laundry basket. *Yes, indeed.* I sighed as I laid the clean sheets across the bed. *Something has got to change.*

WITH BELLS ON, I ENTERED the office and paid my visit to Dr. Myers. He was taken aback at what he saw. "My God, what is happening to you?" He looked at me in disbelief. "Bring me up to speed."

I briefly filled him in on the details. "It seemed to have begun after my visit with you several months ago."

He was taking copious notes as he followed along with my tale of woe. He shifted around on his stool as I wrapped up the discussion. He started with the exam.

"You know, Junior. We are going to get you better starting today." He always spoke with such authority. It was definitely encouraging. "You do not have to live this way, and you will not live this way." He paused as he listened to my heart. "I will just not allow it. You are to report to the x-ray technician's tomorrow morning, and they will be looking closely at your insides."

"What is the point of all this?" I asked. "Doctor, haven't we been through all of this before? Do you really think that these new tests will show us something that we haven't seen or known already?"

His eyes told me that those were "good questions." He had been asked about them before. "I want to confirm that there is blockage in your belly."

"Can't you take my word for it?" I asked in a pleading tone. "Do we really need to take a look up there with your instruments again?"

"I will be frank with you. I am reiterating this point. You are one of the unhealthiest cases I have ever seen. It is a wonder you are alive."

"The FDA has just approved a new drug for such extreme cases as you. I want to put you on it." A chill went down my spine. *Something new. A new hope?* I asked myself. If only it were true. I tried to act cool and control my thoughts.

"Okay." I was willing to do as he asked. The truth was there would be no questions. I was at his whim. "Tell me more about this drug."

THE TESTS DID INDEED CONFIRM Dr. Myer's suspicions. I felt I was like a cat on its last life. Dr. Myer's told me, "Your insides are worse than we could have imagined. But this new drug is called Remicade. It is supposed to be the miracle drug for Crohn's."

He paused. "Let me rephrase this. *It is the* miracle drug for Crohn's."

I couldn't help but interrupt. "When can I begin it?"

He raised his hand. "Slow down. We will cover all of that. Just give me a minute."

I realized that I was getting anxious and ahead of myself. I apologized for cutting him off.

He continued. "You will be my first patient to get this drug. The studies have shown to be very encouraging. It will be given to you through an IV." He pointed to a vein on my hand. "It will take about three to four hours to give you. We will then repeat this process again about once every six weeks."

"How will I know if it works?" All I could think about—the actual possibility of my bellyaches going away.

"To answer your question, you should feel better within twenty-four hours. It is instantaneous."

I could barely stay in my seat as he talked. "But I must warn you ..." *Oh no.* There is always a catch with things that seem too good to be true. "It may not work at all. But I don't think this will happen in your case." That was the typical statement, for insurances purposes I presumed. "The studies have shown that individuals who get this drug can notice a difference almost immediately."

Give me more. Give me more good news. I hadn't heard such encouragement for a while. I was thirsty for it.

"You will start tomorrow. The nurses will fill you in on all of the details. Good Luck."

I thanked him with a handshake. The medicine would be proof in and of itself.

FOR ME, THIS WAS A moment of truth. One drug, one patient, and one last opportunity for a healthy life! There were no other options. Miracles reveal themselves in many different forms. And I needed a miracle.

Remicade had originally been designed to help individuals who were suffering from rheumatoid arthritis. In the process of the studies (as happened with many other drugs before), alternative uses were discovered along the way. In the case of Remicade, or Infliximab by the drug companies, Crohn's patients were responding well to the treatments.

Both arthritis and Crohn's have been classified as autoimmune disorders. In terse laymen's terms, the immune system works *too hard.* In both cases, the immune system is attacking its own body. You could consider it like an overprotective parent. They are watching out for the best interests of the body, though, through the process, the body is being harmed more than it is being helped.

AT DR. MYERS' ORDER, I arrived fifteen minutes early for my scheduled appointment for my first treatment of Remicade. I was taken into a backroom and introduced to several individuals.

Step by step, I was walked through a seemingly long and complex process. Nurse Lynn was the first that I encountered.

"Junior, I will be helping you today. If you have any questions, I will be happy to assist you."

I thanked her. As she was getting me situated, I was overwhelmed by the operations of the infusion center. Having never been in this area of the medical centers, I was simply taking it all in.

As she readied an IV bag, she started to tell me, "Dr. Myers has told us a great deal about you."

I shook my head. "Really?" I had no idea as to why he would talk about me to others.

"I found that out of the ordinary." She stuck me with the needle at that point. I jumped. "Don't worry. That is a natural reaction. What I meant about Dr. Myers is that he has never been one to speak about many of his patients."

"I see. Can I ask you a question about this drug and what you know about it?"

"Sure you can."

"How many individuals do you treat with this? I mean, am I the youngest? I have been familiar with this drug for some time, though I have never actually met another person who has had this or any other form of the illness."

"We do have other patients who are taking Remicade," she stated. "However, they are taking it for arthritis. You are the first person that has been prescribed the Remicade for their Crohn's."

I could just feel the sarcasm bubbling up. I couldn't stop it. "Is there some sort of prize for it?"

"We could make you one," she fired back. "According to the studies I have read, the drug is so new that they are restricting the use of it right now to the most severe of the illness. So congratulations. That means you."

She placed a couple of pills on front of me. "Take these. You need to have a Tylenol and Benadryl prior to us administering the drug."

I asked, "Why is that?" I wasn't quite sure of the reasoning for it.

"Individuals who haven't been given these two pills have been known to have severe allergic reactions." She passed a cup of water so that I could wash the pills down. "Just a precaution," she assured me.

During our conversation, the nurse had gotten the IV running, dripping liquids into my system. She also had the drugs ready to commence. "Watch what I am doing here."

She had my attention.

"This will be dripped over the next four hours. I will give you a small dosage every twenty minutes for the first hour. We will take note of how you react. We just want to make sure that you do not have an allergic reaction. Ring the bell if you need anything." She pushed the bell in front of me and exited the room.

The first dose of the drug went great. It took a little longer than four hours to administer the entire treatment.

"How do you feel?" asked a familiar voice from around the corner. It was Dr. Myers.

"I'm a little tired. I had a few trips to the bathroom in the past few hours. I cannot say, though, that there is a change yet."

"Be patient. You will notice some changes by the end of the week."

I shot him a smile. "I just might have to hold you to that, Doctor."

He pulled up a stool. I could tell he wanted to go over something else. "Junior,"—he put his hand on my knee—"I have to tell you a few possible side effects of this drug."

"I assumed that there would have to be a few." *It was only logical,* I thought.

"Like many new drugs," he began, "there are a good deal of variables and unknowns about Remicade. People will have a wide range of reactions to this medicine, as we all do with all different medications."

I shook my head. "Is there any possible side effect that I should or can concern myself with right now?"

"There is one that we theorize. There is a greater possibility that people who take Remicade for extended periods of time will be more prone to various forms of leukemia. This is only a theory that we have recently developed. It could be years. It could be decades. We do not have the slightest idea."

"Thank you, Doctor." At that point, I couldn't care less. *I'm not going to get cancer.* I laughed at that notion.

He smiled and asked, "Hey Junior, what do you teach?"

"History," I replied.

"Well take a look the calendar before you head out of here today." With that, he slipped out of the room and out of my sight.

On the way out, I saw a newspaper in the waiting room. I leaned over for the front page. *December seventh,* I read to myself, *a day that will live in infamy.*

REMICADE GAVE ME MY LIFE back. Almost instantly, I began to feel rejuvenated. Within a week, my sleeping patterns had improved. I started to sleep through the night for the first time in months. And the intestinal bleeding became less noticeable and the stomach cramps were nonexistent.

And in just two weeks, I had regained nearly ten pounds to my frail frame. My mother said that I was beginning to resemble a healthy human being once again. The color began to return to my face. What had been a look of pale illness had begun to turn back toward a glowing picture of health.

Today, I still get Remicade every six weeks. Like clockwork, I begin to have a flare-up with my bowels, but one infusion of the drug makes most of my ills go away almost immediately. It is a miracle!

CHAPTER 11

I put the book down and felt my chest.

AS A YOUNG TENNIS PLAYER, I would often just walk onto the court and try to hit the ball harder than my opponent. I was completely unprepared to compete and frequently ended up losing. I was just as unprepared for dealing with the Crohn's disease, the accidents and upset stomachs. I was too young and immature to handle either appropriately.

I have grown up a great deal because of my experiences both on and off the tennis court. Today when I take the tennis court, I study the environmental conditions: the heat, the wind, and the sun. Which way is the wind blowing? Where is the sun in the sky? Will it be in my eyes?

And I learned to study my opponent too. Which hand does he hit with? Is it a two-handed or one-handed backhand? As I've gotten better, I have learned how to quickly study all of these factors and determine the best way by which to approach the match and deal with the circumstances facing me. I've become a better player as I have learned how to adapt.

I've also used these experiences to better cope with this incurable, but very manageable disease. Before I go on a long road trip, I research where the rest stops are located. As I have driven up and down the highways, I've learned what exits have what bathrooms, which ones are usually clean, and which ones are most accessible. These have become regular practices because my frequent bowel movements have been known to be like lightening; sudden, unexpected, and shocking.

I also carry extra clothing with me where ever I go out. My car, my classroom, and my parent's house all have extra shorts, shirts, socks and most importantly, underwear. Even for a simple overnighter, I carry at least three pairs of underwear. I don't have enough fingers to tell you how many times that I've needed an extra pair of underwear.

THE MOST SIGNIFICANT LESSON I'VE learned from my Crohn's has been how attune I've become with my body over the years. I've never been one to rush off to the doctor for every little ache or pain, but I've come to know my body well enough to know when something wasn't quite right.

Once I had been on Remicade for six months and was stronger, the Crohn's was under control, however,

I started to feel differently. I might not know what the problem was, but I was tuned in enough to my body to know that something wasn't right.

I woke up one May morning and my groin was throbbing. I reached down to scratch myself and felt a harder, tender testicle. *Not normal,* I thought to myself.

So I decided to call Kaiser to schedule an appointment. I pulled out the telephone book to make the call. I was hoping that I could get a same-day appointment, though I knew that the chances of that were not too likely. As I thumbed the pages, I thought of the unbearable throbbing over and over again. I shifted from side to side as I stood up against the counter. With each beat of my heart, I had this vision of my groin getting more and more swollen.

I dialed the number and waited. One ring, two rings, three rings.

"Kaiser San Rafael; how may I direct your call?"

"Could I arrange an appointment with an urologist? I'm having a problem with my ... my lower parts." *So awkward and embarrassing.*

The voice on the other side replied, "May I have your medical record number?"

I gave the number and asked, "When is the next available appointment?"

"Let me see."

The pause on the phone was beginning to make me uncomfortable. The more time that passed, the more freaked out I was becoming. Something was wrong, and I couldn't figure it out.

"My next available appoint is with Dr. Forrester on Friday, June 13th. Would you like to come in then?"

My God! "A month?" I wasn't sure this could wait a month. This is exactly why so many people have had such negative experiences with Kaiser. "Yes, I'll take it." What bothered me most was the seemingly lack of concern in the voice of this receptionist. I was just another number.

I thought that it was absolutely unacceptable that I was going to have to wait over one month before an appointment. *What the hell is that about?* I expect and, moreover, demand service when I am paying the bills. I hung up the phone and stood in the kitchen for a minute, mulling over my options. *What to do? What to do?* I thought of my father. "There is always more than one way to solve a problem, Junior." At that moment, I got an idea.

I picked up the phone and dialed a number that I had been given only in cases of emergencies. The number was Dr. Myers' direct line to his office. He stressed, "Only use this if you think there is an emergency." And when I think about the labyrinth that the Kaiser phone system is, I knew that having his direct line was a godsend.

Little did I know my next call would save my life!

He rarely picked up the phone because of his busy schedule, but he was great about calling back in an expedient fashion. I just had a feeling that he would be able to help me out. This was my answer to solving my problem. Dr. Myers was my biggest advocate.

After it went to his voice mail, I left a terse message: "Dr. Myers, it's Junior. I was calling because I need your help. I need to see a urologist. I've only been able to get an appointment for a month from now. I don't think this can wait. Please help."

I had placed extra emphasis with my voice on the phrase *please help*. I hung up the phone feeling better and more confident knowing that I had contacted him.

With nothing else I could do but wait, I tried to keep my mind occupied. I sat down to read a book.

Forty-five minutes later, the phone rang.

"Hello," I said.

The voice on the other line was both familiar and relieving.

"Junior, Dr. Myers here. I got your message. I wanted to let you know that you have an appointment with Dr. Alperts this afternoon at 3:00 p.m."

"Thank you. Thank you, Doctor." Grateful wouldn't even have begun to describe my feelings.

"You let me know what happens today. You got that?"

"Yes, sir!" I clicked the phone off and stole a glance at the kitchen clock. Three o'clock. *Only two hours to go.*

WHAT A RELIEF. I WENT back to my reading. I had come across a copy of *It's Not About the Bike* by Lance Armstrong a week earlier, and I had become engrossed in his story.

I was reading a passage about his diagnosis, and I

was becoming unnerved by what I was reading. "Do your nipples hurt?" read one passage.

I put the book down and felt my chest. Mine did. *Were things going to be all right?* I put my hands on my nipples; they were swollen too. My spine began to tingle as I became full of fright.

There was a feeling of nausea that hit me deep in the pit of my stomach. I wanted to vomit, so I sprinted to the bathroom as I'd done so many times before. Nothing! My thoughts shifted from fear to denial. *There is no way that this is happening! It isn't possible.* I wasn't convinced though. *There's got to be a logical explanation.*

I started to read a bit further in the book. Sadly, as I read more and more, I became more convinced that I was in trouble. I couldn't control my feelings anymore. I started to cry. I had to stop reading. I began to slowly accept my fate. I knew my body well enough to know this wasn't a mistake.

At that moment, my mind, my body, and my soul accepted the worst: Cancer.

I HAD NEVER FELT AS alone in this world as I did during the thirty-minute drive to my appointment. I entered the doctor's office with my medical card in one hand and my copy of Lance's book clutched in my other hand. I was still hoping for the best, but I was ready for the worst.

A nurse stuck her head through the door. "Junior Street," she called.

I got up and met hear at the door.

"Right this way, young man. We are first going to have to get your measurements, your weight, and height."

Stepping on to the scale, I began to adjust the scale, knowing that my weight was approximately 180 pounds. It was back up to its healthy range. *I feel good and healthy*. I was having difficulty wrapping my mind around the idea of cancer.

The nurse guided me down the hall into an examination room. "So, what are you here for today?" she asked quizzically.

I hesitated before saying, "I have a swollen testicle. I would rather wait for the doctor, if you don't mind."

"Okay," she replied. Folding up my chart, she exited the room and said, "The doctor will be with you shortly."

AFTER WHAT SEEMED TO BE a wait of considerable time, there came a knock at the examination door. *The moment of truth*, I thought. The door opened ever so slowly.

"Hello. My name is Dr. Alperts."

Shaking hands after our introduction, I started off on my diatribe, explaining how I had discovered something wrong and how long I had been showing signs of the symptoms.

He listened intently, taking notes without interruption. Once I finished, he started. "Well, let's start with a basic examination." I stood up and dropped my shorts.

He proceeded to inspect my groin noticing the

swollen right testicle and comparing it to its counterpart on the left.

"Now, what I want you to do is go ahead and put your shorts back on and sit back on the table with your shirt off."

I followed his instructions, and he began to check various points on my body. Pressing on my hips and groin, I learned later that he was feeling some of my lymph nodes.

"Does that hurt?" he asked.

As he pressed on my chest, I flinched. "Yes, it does," I stated. "For some strange reason, it feels swollen too."

"Well, can you recall how long you have felt that way?"

"I don't know. A couple of months maybe."

He reached for my medical file and scribbled a few notes down. "Why don't you get dressed and meet me in my office. It's right around the corner."

My heart was racing. I was afraid of what he was going to say. I was also afraid of what he wasn't going to say. I put my shirt on and walked out of the exam room into his office two doors away. It was empty, so I double checked the name placard before entering. I took a seat in front of his oak desk and waited.

A knock at the door rattled my eardrums. I swiveled in my chair to see that Dr. Alperts had entered the room, removing his white coat. He took his seat across from me, setting a file folder on his desktop, neatly in line with all of the others.

"Junior, you're lucky that you got here when you did." There was a long pause. He made himself comfortable, pulling himself toward the edge of his desk. His chair squeaked as he reached across his desk for one of the other file folders.

He leaned forward and opened the folder and glanced at it briefly before setting it back in line with the others.

My heart raced.

"Junior, you have cancer."

"No! No!" I shouted. I leaned back in my chair in disbelief. I felt a sudden pain in my gut. I hunched over, placing my left hand on the desk for support. Stunned, I tried to catch my breath. I sat back up in my chair breathless.

He came over to help me. "Junior," he said, "try to catch your breath. Things are going to be all right. I'm here to help you."

With his help, I was able to recollect my thoughts. I shook my head and wiped away a tear that was forming in my eye.

His blue eyes stared intently into mine. "Junior, this is a very treatable disease."

I stared at his forehead as he began to talk. I knew he was talking because I watched his lips move, and I heard his words rolling toward me in slow motion. But I had stopped listening. I just couldn't. I wanted to put my fingers in my ears. I gripped the arms of my chair as if the chair was my lifeline. The doctor sounded garbled, like he was talking under water.

I shut my eyes to find a safe haven just for a moment away from his bad news. My mind took me to a distant land to a future that I didn't fully recognize.

I AM STANDING AT THE top of a steep hill in front of my childhood home. The house looked more worn than I ever noticed before. The trim looked like it had been chipped away by years of wind and rain, but I could still see the horrible shade of blue that my mother loved so immensely.

I quickly walked toward the house, ecstatic to see my family. The grinding of the gravel under my feet reminded me of the many times I walked home from school happy to be safe in my family home. The driveway was full of cars. *That was nothing unusual.* Our family was famous or infamous in our neighborhood for our boisterous gatherings. With a family of seven children, our family gatherings were more like an event.

Quickening my pace, I started toward the front door. When I reached the lawn, I stopped under the shade of the giant elm tree and looked straight up at the top of it. It was as if it was touching the sky. *How did it that gets so big so quickly? Dad and I just planted it last summer.* I brought my attention away from the tree and turned my attention to the large window in the front of the house. My parents, siblings, nieces, and nephews were all gathered around the dining room table. *Like the house and the tree, they all looked different.*

I didn't want to miss out. I dashed up the three steps leading to the front door. Entering the house, I announced, "Hello, everyone. I'm sorry that I'm late."

No one responded, as if I hadn't said anything. They acted as if they didn't even know I was there.

I was there, wasn't I?

The room was filled with laughter and love. It felt like a family holiday at our home.

I walked up behind my father at the head of the table, when my older sister, Katee, came out of the kitchen holding a chocolate cake topped with whipped cream, my *favorite.* She walked delicately to the table with one arm covering the candles to protect the flame from extinguishing. "One, two, three," she said, and my family began to sing. "Happy birthday to you. Happy birthday to you." *Whose birthday is it?* After Katee centered the cake on the table, she stepped away as the song concluded. "Happy birthday, dear, Junior. Happy birthday to you." Two blue candles sat in the middle of the whipped cream and stood out like two beacons, "5–0." *But I wasn't fifty years old. I was just a couple of days shy of my twenty-fifth birthday.*

I leaned over my father's right shoulder to blow out the candles. I drew in a giant breath, exhaled, and then *whoosh;* nothing happened. The laughter, the clapping, and the celebration slipped into silence. The candles continued to burn.

My mother was crying. Across the table, my older brother put his arm around her. The candles lit the tears to be seen rolling down her cheeks. The rest of the family huddled closer to her, arms around one another. She began to speak. "I can't believe it. I can't believe it's been twenty-five years."

"We know, Mom," one of my brothers said. "It's hard on all of us."

"Junior would've been fifty today." She buried her face in her hands.

Everyone inched closer to comfort her.

I watched the rest of the night unfold from a distance. The candles burned, no birthday cake was eaten, no birthday wishes were made, and no presents were unwrapped.

I was left alone to wonder what might have been.

I OPENED MY EYES AS I was shaken on my shoulder. Dr. Alperts was leaning across his desk with his right hand clenching my left shoulder.

"Junior, did you get all that?"

"Huh?" I replied. "Sorry, Doctor. I'm overwhelmed." He slid a couple of sheets of paper across his desk toward me. "I'm sorry. What are these for again?"

He handed me the top sheet—"This is for the blood tests at the lab,"—and then the second sheet—"and this is for the x-ray."

"X-ray?" I asked.

"Yes, we need to assess the situation." He paused. "This will tell us if the cancer has spread."

"Spread?" Cancer itself was dreadful; the notion that it could be spreading through my body was outright unimaginable. "How will I know? What if it has spread? What're we going to do?" Each question was fired in rapid succession, without giving the doctor an opportunity to respond. I started to feel weak again. *Is the room spinning?* I was starting to lose control.

"There's nothing else to do at the moment," he stated. "We have to take this one step at a time."

As I stood up, he held out his hand. He reassured me.

"Junior this is the most treatable of cancers. You can beat this."

I nodded and quietly headed toward the door.

"See you Monday."

I turned back over my shoulder. "Monday?"

"Yes. That last sheet there has all of the instructions." He pointed toward my book. We're going to operate on Monday to remove the tumor."

"Right. See you then." That was one of the many things I must've missed as I tuned out there slightly.

AFTER LEAVING KAISER IN SAN Rafael that fateful day, I hopped in my car and headed back home. In afternoon traffic, it was approximately forty-five minutes.

Driving in somewhat of a daze, I flipped the radio on to the local pop hits. The radio was simply for background noise. I tried to turn up the music loud enough to drown out the negative thoughts from my mind. No luck.

I tried to come to grips with my own mortality and deal with Bay Area traffic all at once. As I approached the last leg of my trip home, the song, "Soak Up the Sun" by Sheryl Crow came on the radio. With its upbeat tempo and catchy lyrics, I began to sing along. Her song helped me clear my mind that afternoon.

It didn't chase away all of the fear for me, but it did help set me toward the necessary frame of mind I was going to need to survive this ordeal.

I knew then deep down that I would be all right.

CHAPTER 12

I was one of those seven thousand young men.

PERHAPS THE ONLY THING I can think of that is worse than being told that I had cancer was breaking the news to my loved ones. *How do I share this with them?* I wasn't sure that there was a special way, so I simply figured the truth was best. I couldn't handle the commuter traffic, so I pulled off the freeway to find a pay phone. The first person that I confided with was my older brother, Steven, living in Illinois.

"I need to talk with you."

I've always hated sharing my problems with others. I never thought it was fair that others should have to bear the burden of my struggles, especially telling my brother this type of news when he was so distant from me; there wasn't anything that he could do. And like me, he has always had the propensity of trying to help and fix things when someone he cared about had a problem. There was little that could be done.

"I just came from a doctor's appointment."

"Is anything *wrong?*" I could feel the concern in his voice.

"Yes. I was just told I have a tumor on my right testicle." Silence filled the miles between us. "It is cancer; testicular cancer, just like the biker, Lance Armstrong."

"Oh, buddy, I'm so sorry."

I can't say who felt more helpless at that point, me or my brother.

I proceeded to fill him in on the details. At that point, the only thing on my mind was the impending surgery, which was five days away.

"I took a blood test, chest x-ray, and the doctor is going to operate on Monday."

We said good bye to each other and I got back into my car to head home.

I DECIDED THAT I WAS going to wait until everyone got home and had settled in for the evening. Since I had come back from my negative college experience, I had lived at home with my parents and younger siblings. I would be the first one to admit that I'm quite the homebody. I was a week away from my twenty-fifth birthday and still living with my parents.

IT WAS AROUND 9:00 P.M. when I finally had built up the courage to start talking. All evening, I tried to keep a positive attitude and pretend that nothing was wrong. I think it worked because neither of my parents or siblings asked me about anything.

My father had assumed his usual position, the end seat on the couch watching the Wednesday line-up. Like clockwork, he would be up for another couple of hours, following his routine of a bath between the hours of ten and eleven and then back down on the couch to watch the eleven o'clock news on CBS. He was a very by the book person.

We never really exchanged a whole lot in terms of personal conversation. I knew I was going to be uncomfortable speaking to him about this, also knowing that he was going to be just us uncomfortable. So I decided to tell my mother first, figuring and hoping that she would be the one to break the news to him. I got up from the couch and headed back upstairs to talk with my mother.

Having just put in hardwood floors, my steps echoed throughout the family room as I made the climb. I could hear Mom shuffling around with papers or a book perhaps. Entering the room, she was just where I assumed that she would be: under the covers, reading a book, trying to correct some papers and squeeze in her nightly fix of television at an unreasonably high volume. We always joked that she wanted everyone to hear the show from all over the house.

"How was your day?" she fired at me. "You're home early," she stated.

"Mom, it's Wednesday. I have class on Tuesdays." I reached for the remote to hit the mute button.

"Oh yeah. It is Wednesday, isn't it?"

"Yes, Mom." I rolled my eyes and took a deep breath. "I have to tell you something." I was on the verge of tears. "I went to Kaiser today for a checkup. The doctor told me I have a tumor. He is going to operate on Monday." *There. I did it. What a relief. Speak, Mom. Say something.*

She broke the silence. Slamming the book down, she tersely responded the way only my mother could. "Oh my God." I could see the anger and frustration in her face.

My mother began to cry. "Are you sure? How do you know?"

"I felt something odd yesterday, and I went to Kaiser." I sat on the bed and held her hand. "They're certain. I'm having surgery Monday."

"No, no, no." She shook her head. "This just can't be. You're healthy once again. This has to be wrong."

"It isn't. It has to be done," I declared.

I knew it was difficult to accept. Mom had always been my biggest advocate and worried constantly the previous seven years of my life about the Crohn's disease.

We all had thought I'd turned a corner for the better. That was the frustrating part. My stomach began to settle, my bowels relaxed, color had returned to my face, and weight started to stick. And now this? Terrible.

I stood up from her bed and stepped back. "Mom,

things will be all right. I'm going to go to the library tomorrow to do a little research, and we can figure out what needs to be done. Okay?"

"Okay." She wiped away a tear. "Have you told anyone else about this?"

"Just Steve. I called him this afternoon once I got the news."

"What about Tiffany?"

I took a deep breath. "Not yet." I dropped my shoulders and tried to relax. "I'm going to give her a call next."

"Okay." She sat up from her bed and motioned me toward her. "I won't say anything except to your father, until we hear more news."

I hugged her, and she gave me a kiss good night. I headed back to my room to make the call to Tiffany. I heard my mother break out in tears as I shut the door to her bedroom.

I dialed her number, and Tiffany answered right away. We'd been together for nearly five years after we met in junior college. Tiffany was at her parent's house in the east bay in the small town of Lafayette.

The phone call was somewhat of a nightly ritual the nights she didn't stay in Petaluma with me at my parent's house.

"Hi, Junior," she said in her ever cheery tone. "How was your day?"

"Oh, it was fine. Nothing special." I spoke carefully, trying to find the opening for the bad news. "Tiffany, I have some bad news."

The hesitation in my thought was broken when she interjected, "What is it? Is there something wrong?"

"I went to the doctor today and was diagnosed with cancer."

"Junior, don't joke like that. It isn't funny."

I was always a joker, so this was a legitimate reaction for her.

"I'm not. I'll be fine. They're operating on Monday to remove the tumor." I didn't hear any tears, and her tone was all right.

"Tumor?" she asked. "Things can't be good if there is a tumor."

"Don't worry, baby. It will be all right, okay? I promise." I started to hear the sniffles. Her tears were sure to fall. I hated to hear her cry.

"Okay." She tried to not cry. "Are you sure? I can't live without you."

"Why don't you come over tomorrow, and we can talk more about it?"

"Okay, honey." She cried some more. I just listened, feeling helpless. I was quickly realizing that this illness was going to take just as much of an emotional and psychological toll on my family as it was on me.

Tiffany was finally able to collect herself, and we were able to resume our conversation. We were able to chat about a few other things that evening. We talked about the baseball game. The Oakland A's had won their third game in a row. I finally said good night and went to bed.

I crawled under the covers and closed my eyes. I reached under my shorts and held the tumor. It was a rock. *This is going to kill me,* I thought. *Unbelievable!*

I WOKE UP THE NEXT day refreshed, feeling a little less scared. I was still in shock as I ran through a brief timeline in my head. Monday, I was feeling strong and healthy. Tuesday, I felt a lump. Wednesday, I got cancer. And now, next Monday, I was having surgery. What a week, and it was only Thursday, May 16. I had plenty of time to fill until Monday the 20th.

I stayed home from work to do research, trying to gain a greater perspective on my predicament. I sat down at my parent's antiquated computer from the year 2000. To add insult to my impatience, they were still using a dial-up modem to log onto the Web. I logged on and trudged through the Internet.

I found what I was looking for early in my search. The website I found was perfect: "The Testicular Cancer Resource Center." I wanted to know why I needed blood tests and a chest x-ray. I discovered that the cancer could be measured with a simple blood test, along with the x-ray, which could determine if the cancer spread at all.

It broke the illness down into its respective stages—types of cancer—and into its various treatments. I learned a good deal that day about cancer, chemotherapy, as well as a lot of misnomers. As I took in this information, I was comforted by the knowledge that my mind was ingesting. The information was allowing me to get past my worst fear: death. The success stories of the survivors provided me with precious peace of mind.

I concluded that I had to sit tight and wait for the surgery and the test results to ascertain the severity of the disease.

Everything I read on the Internet said that testicular cancer was the best, most treatable cancer. Approximately seven thousand young men are diagnosed with the disease each year. Having no reference to compare that number to, I pulled up statistics on another cancer. I found a statistic about colon cancer. According the current cancer statistics, there were about one hundred thousand new colon cancer cases each year. Despite that, this information was an eye-opener for me, I was still, unfortunately, one of those seven thousand young men.

I was also relieved to read that even in the worst of cases, it was still very treatable. Of those seven thousand diagnoses each year, only about four hundred die. It was dependent on how soon it was caught. I hoped I wasn't one of the four hundred. I hoped we caught it early.

CHAPTER 13

A real thread of hope.

I WAITED FOUR LONG DAYS in solemn thought and near isolation, waiting for the surgery. It was Monday, May 20th, that Dr. Alperts had scheduled for the operation. That morning, I was supposed to be at the hospital by nine in the morning. I rode down to San Rafael with Tiffany. It was a day surgery, so I was going to be home by the early afternoon.

The procedure was to take about an hour. We arrived at the hospital and checked in with the station nurse. Tiffany and I followed her up to the procedure room where I was to be prepped prior to surgery.

As we sat in the waiting room, Tiffany and I held hands in silence. I tried to thumb through a magazine, but I couldn't concentrate. I looked at Tiffany, and she asked, "What are you thinking?"

Tiffany had a habit of asking that question. I gave her the usual reply: "Nothing much."

"Oh, okay." She reached for a copy of *Vogue* magazine that sat on the table. My thoughts were carrying me back to the four years earlier when I had been operated on for the colitis. I was thinking of the drastic differences between the two surgeries.

I was so hopeful back then sitting in the exact same waiting room with Tiffany and my parents. I laughed under my breath a bit.

Tiffany heard me. "What is so funny, Junior?"

"I was just thinking of the irony here."

"What do you mean?"

"Well, do you remember the last time we were here?" I asked.

She didn't say anything right away, but said, "That's right. When you had surgery on your stomach." She paused. "Why did you say ironic though?"

"Well, that surgery was supposed to make me healthy and give me my life back"—I motioned my hands in the air in frustration—"and now"—I paused—"Here we are again, and I'm dying."

"I know, honey. I know."

"This sucks, Tiffany." I hated to complain, but I felt a little better sharing my frustrations.

Our conversation was broken up by a nurse, who came to retrieve me for surgery.

"Junior Street." She glanced around the waiting room.

We both stood up, and the nurse led me and Tiffany to the back area of the hospital.

I was excused to get undressed and get on the infamous hospital gown. I had never imagined I'd have to go through any operation again. I was in the dressing room and came back out with my clothes in one hand and one hand holding the backside of my gown.

I tried to lighten the mood. "How do I look, Tiff?" I spun around like a model with my backside hanging out.

She was seated in a chair right next to the bed that I was supposed to get into. "You look great, Junior." She smiled. I leaned forward and kissed her.

The nurse came back and introduced herself. "Hello, Junior. I'm Debbie, and I'm going to help get you situated before the doctor comes in to see you."

"Nice to meet you." I motioned toward Tiffany. "This is my girlfriend, Tiffany."

"Hello, Tiffany." She extended her hand. "So I assume that you will be driving Junior home after the procedure?"

"Yep. I will be."

"Let's get started then." I heard the snap of her rubber gloves against her skin. "I've got to start an IV, and then we need to go over this checklist." She pointed to her clipboard.

"How long will this take?" I asked.

"Once we get this set up, it will be about ten minutes before we wheel you into the operating room."

"Good," I said. "I'm getting a bit nervous."

"I understand," and I flinched as she stuck my right hand with a needle. I hadn't even realized that she had done that.

I looked at Tiffany as she reacted to my sudden movement. We watched as Nurse Debbie set up the IV line and got the fluids dripping. Then she grabbed her clipboard.

"Now Junior, I need to double check all of your information and go over the type of procedure that we'll be doing today."

"Your name is?" She waited for my response.

"Wayne Street, Jr." I replied. "Date of birth is May 23rd, 1977."

She reached for my wrist and looked at my tag. "I need to double check your medical record number." I watched her lips move as she mouthed the nine-digit number. I had come to memorize the number myself, like a soldier who could recite his name, rank, and serial number. "And, lastly, we're operating on your right side today to remove the tumor?"

"Correct," I replied.

"Would you point to your right leg please?"

I was a bit confused. "Excuse me?"

"Your right leg; point to it."

I reached down to my right leg.

"Very good, Junior. I'll go get the doctor." As she walked away, she pulled the curtain closed again to give me and Tiffany some privacy.

We held hands and waited in nervous anticipation. Silence. There wasn't much to say. The curtain was pulled back swiftly. Tiffany jumped.

"Junior, how are you doing today?" Dr. Alperts stood at the foot of the bed in his scrubs.

"I'm doing okay." I extended my hand to him. "This is my girlfriend, Tiffany."

"Tiffany, nice to meet you." He moved along the side of the bed to address us. "Junior, I wanted to let you know that this will be a relatively simple procedure." I nodded. "The procedure itself is nothing more than a simple hernia operation." He pulled out a pen and pushed my gown up my right leg. "We will be making a three-inch slice in your groin, and I'll just reach in there and pull out the testicle. Do either of you have any questions?"

"Won't you look around?" I asked. "What if the cancer is elsewhere?"

"There won't be any need to look around."

"Why not?" I was concerned.

"That is why we did the blood test and x-ray last week. I'll be able to see if the tumor is encased or not. That'll be an indicator. Other than that, we'll wait for the tests."

"How long will all of this take?" interjected Tiffany.

"Once we get started, we should be rolling Junior back out of the operating room within forty-five to sixty minutes."

I clapped my hands together and said, "Okay, Doctor. Let's get to this then. I'm ready."

"One last thing, Junior." He pulled out a black felt marker. "What side are we operating on?"

I hesitated.

"This is how we confirm the accuracy of the procedure. Check twice, cut once, I always say."

I thought of the possibilities. *One testicle? No tes-*

ticles? I pointed to my right leg and groin area. Just like a construction worker who measures twice and cut once, Dr. Alperts took the marker and wrote an "X" on my right quadriceps.

He turned around toward Nurse Debbie. "We're ready."

Tiffany stood up and kissed me good-bye as the nurse came around the back of the bed to start rolling me away. I waved to Tiffany and kept my eyes on her until she was out of sight.

I was greeted by another doctor. "Hello, Junior. Here is your three-drug cocktail." It was the anesthesiologist. I watched as he held his needle up in front of me just before he knocked me out.

That anesthesia was amazing. I could feel myself slipping away for an instant, but I tried to fight it, only to awake seemingly moments later in the recovery room. Surgery was over.

As I came to, I heard the beeping of the heart monitor measure the rhythm of my pulse. Objects started to come into focus, I recognized Tiffany immediately. She sat on the foot of my bed wiggling my toes as I was regaining my bearings.

I saw a figure next to her. It was Dr. Alperts. "Junior, I have good news."

I tried to sit up a bit.

"Everything went as planned. The tumor was totally encased. We are shipping the tumor off to the lab as soon as we possibly can." He smiled. "They will run a few tests and give us detailed information on the types of cancer that you have."

I smiled at him, high from the anesthesia.

"With the tumor completely encased, the chances of the cancer having spread are remote."

"Great." I struggled for the words. I reached out, and he held my hand. "Thanks, Doctor."

It took another fifteen to twenty minutes for me to get my head cleared. Tiffany sat by my side, and I felt her hand resting on my foot. And Nurse Debbie checked on me every ten minutes or so for the next hour. As my head became clearer, the throbbing and the burning sensation in my groin began to grow.

The early news from the doctor had been good—a *real thread of hope*. After about an hour in the recovery room, I was ready to start the healing process and go home. With the tumor gone, I thought my health could improve and all the doctor had to do was monitor me for some period of time.

Nurse Debbie went over release procedures with Tiffany, along with prescriptions for the pain. Aw, Vicodin, the end-all, cure-all wonder drug for pain. After helping me get dressed through the fog, I shifted gingerly on the bed, trying to get comfortable. Nurse Debbie told Tiffany that she could go get the car. "I'll wheel Junior down to the main entrance for you."

Tiffany thanked her and left.

I was seated upright on the bed ready. "Nurse Debbie, I'm ready to get going when you are." She brought over a wheelchair and said, "Why don't you take a seat here, and I'll take you down to the entry where Tiffany is."

I took one look at the chair and told the nurse,

"Debbie, I walked into this hospital, and I'll be walking out too." I stood up quickly and took one strong step and then stumbled. Losing my footing, I fell to the ground.

In that brief moment on the ground, I realized that this was going to be harder than I'd anticipated. It was going to be a journey that I could not take alone. This fall to the ground was just a prelude of the struggles ahead of me.

CHAPTER 14

My precious hair…

THREE DAYS AFTER THE SURGERY, my family helped me celebrate my twenty-fifth birthday. It was a solemn occasion, almost subdued. I had gotten over the genuine fear of the circumstances, but I was still overwhelmed with all the different thoughts that were going through my head.

Early in the afternoon, my mother had taken me to Kaiser again for a CAT scan. The scan was supposed to give the doctor a better look inside to see if there was any cancer in the other parts of my body. It was a surreal moment as I lay flat on my back on a table as the machine scanned for disease.

After the CAT scan, my mother drove me home and took me to a fast food place for dinner: Chuncky's. It was a new restaurant at the time and was the latest craze with all of the locals. I remember I ordered a torta. It was a pretty good dish, but it didn't taste as good under the circumstances.

We took our meal down to the tennis club to eat on the deck. It was a warm night, one that wouldn't blow us away with the famous Petaluma wind. As we sat down, we were visited by my many friends and fellow members of the tennis club. The news was still under wraps.

"Hello, Junior. How's it going?" someone asked.

"I'm doing fine. Thank you." I would usually continue, "How's the tennis game tonight?"

That night was the first time I started to confide in a few of my friends at the club. I saw the owner, Rob, and we got to talking for a moment and I told him the news.

I also told my buddy, John. They both offered their best wishes and thoughts and prayers. That was all I could've asked for anyways.

THE DAY OF THE POST-OP appointment with Dr. Alperts finally arrived four days after my birthday. My family and I had waited in agony for a week, for the day to arrive. I went back to Kaiser to meet with the doctor, and Tiffany came with me again to sit at my side and learn what the next step was.

We were taken into see Dr. Alperts almost immediately upon our arrival, and we took our seats across from him. He began by checking on how I was feeling after the surgery. I had told him that I felt as if I had been recovering just fine.

"Junior, I've reviewed everything," he began, "the blood, the x-rays, the CT scan, and the pathology of the tumor. You indeed have testicular cancer called non-seminona."

"How bad is it?"

"As I told you both last week, the tumor was encased."

I interjected, "That is good, isn't it?"

"Absolutely, unfortunately, your cancer has spread."

Spread? I reached out and grabbed Tiffany's hand. I felt I was just sucker-punched in the gut.

"Oh, dear God," I said. "Are you sure?"

"We're sure," he said as he passed me a sheet of paper. "Take a look at these numbers here. Do you see them?" I nodded. "These are called tumor markers. In a healthy male, this number should be less than 5. When you took the blood test last week, it was 25,678."

I gasped. "What does that mean?"

"Well, this puts you in stage two for this cancer. There are three stages for testicular cancer."

"Am I going to die?" I had been dying to ask that question, no pun intended.

"I don't think so, but you will need some treatments."

"Treatments?" I swallowed. "Do you mean chemotherapy?"

"I'm afraid so." I ran my fingers through my hair—my precious hair.

"There is a bit of good news though."

I sat back up to listen.

"The tumor marker has a half life of forty-eight hours, meaning that number should be cut in half every two days."

"So the number has gone down? Does that mean the cancer is going away?"

"Yes and no." He showed us another sheet of paper. On the follow-up blood test, the numbers dropped, but on the second test, it started to rise again. This means that the cancer is elsewhere in your body," he said, waving his pen up and down at my torso.

"So, when do we start then?" I didn't want to waste any time.

"Next week," he said quickly.

"Is there anything else that I need to do before I start chemotherapy?"

"There is one other thing."

I waited as he took a moment.

"I don't mean to intrude, but I presume that your relationship is pretty serious."

Tiffany jumped in. "We've been together for five years. This guy just hasn't gotten around to proposing to me yet." She smiled at me and leaned closer. I had been feeling the pressure for some time now, and this ordeal was only adding to it.

"Junior, I think that you should be considering going to a sperm bank."

"Excuse me?" I replied definitely caught off-guard.

"You see, chemotherapy will defeat all fast-dividing cells, sperm cells being one of them. In all likelihood, you will be left sterile from these treatments."

I wasn't sure what to think. We had talked about

marriage, but now I was discussing my future children before a very uncertain future.

"Thanks for the heads-up, Doctor. I'll look into it."

"Just so you know, Junior, you will be starting your chemotherapy next week, so this would need to be done this week."

"I understand. Thank you, Doctor."

He excused us and walked us out of the office back to the lobby.

Just what I needed, another thing to do this week—a bank deposit. Children? What a far off thought.

CHAPTER 15

A nurse, a magazine, and a cup

AFTER MY TALK WITH DR. Alperts, I went online and researched fertility clinics. Every site I reviewed strongly encouraged testicular cancer patients to use a fertility clinic prior to undergoing chemotherapy. The thought of doing this had never dawned on me.

MY RESEARCH LED ME TO a clinic in San Francisco. I contacted them early one afternoon, and I explained my quandary to the pleasant receptionist who promised to me with all of my banking needs.

"I'll be more than happy to assist you, Mr. Street."

I bet she will assist me. "Mr. Street, we can schedule you an appointment over the phone. When you come in, you can complete all of the necessary paperwork and then leave your donation."

"That seems simple enough." I laughed to myself. "When can we get all of this taken care of?"

"How about in two days?" she asked.

"Yeah. That will work." I recorded the appointment on the calendar and asked, "Is there anything else I need to know or do prior to the visit?"

"Yes. You need to abstain from sex and/or an orgasm for forty-eight hours prior to your appointment."

I thought about her comment and replied, "So I cannot do anything between now and then?"

"Actually, an optimal sperm count will be achieved when you have no more or less than forty-eight hours between ejaculations."

I couldn't believe she said that word—the *e* word. This conversation went from embarrassing to uncomfortable to weird.

"So, what are you saying then?" I asked. "Should I have a *release* tonight?"

"Yes, you should," she said in a matter-of-fact tone.

"Well, thank you very much. You have answered all of my questions and then some." I said good-bye and hung up the phone.

Thinking about my situation, I called Tiffany and replayed the entire conversation to me. We laughed and laughed. She wasn't going to be around that evening to help me.

Once again, I found myself on my own!

TWO DAYS LATER AS I was getting ready to leave for the clinic, the phone rang; it was my buddy, Joey. "What're you doing?" the voice said.

"Nothing, right now," I said. "I'm headed to the bank in a couple of hours. That's all."

"Want some company?"

Happy to have the company, I accepted his offer. "Sure. I was going to leave in about an hour. I gotta be there at 4:00 p.m."

"Okay. I'll pick you up at three."

I hung up the phone. I was feeling better. I sat in the living room on one of my mother's blue chairs. I stared on the window, waiting for Joey. He pulled into the driveway with his Passat.

I bolted out the door, double-checking that I had my wallet, money, and my ID. Getting into the car, Joey threw a package into my lap. "I got you a little gift."

"What the hell is it?" I perused over the brown bag. "Nice wrap job."

"Bite me," he said with sarcasm in his voice. "I just thought that it would help to get you focused."

Opening up the package, I had a hunch what was inside. "Thanks." I began laughing as I turn through the pages of two *Hustler* magazines. I hadn't seen any in a good period of time.

"This should do the trick," he said in a matter-of-fact manner. "I expect you to make a good-size deposit today."

As we rolled down highway 101 into San Francisco, I flipped through the magazines, laughing at the ridiculous poses. "Oh, look at this one," I exclaimed to Joey as I held the magazine up in front of him. He swerved, and I pulled the magazine down.

"Dude, I'm trying to drive here," he said. "Just keep looking at those."

We both laughed.

A few minutes went by, and I looked out to my right as a suburban passed us by. I caught the driver, who must have been about forty years old, looking in at our car and seeing what magazine I had. We made eye contact, and he smiled.

His car passed us by. I told Joey, "Quick. Speed up to the suburban, will you?" I felt the car jolt forward as he hit the gas. As we approached the suburban, I opened up the magazine and pressed it against my window in the passenger's seat.

"What the hell are you doing?" Joey shouted.

As Joey spoke, I was laughing at the driver's reaction. He laughed and smiled as his car veered slightly into our lane, narrowly avoiding a collision with us.

"Stop it, Junior. He almost hit us."

"Relax," I said.

Looking back, he gave me the thumbs up. Then I noticed his wife in the passenger's seat discovered what the source of his distraction was. Judging by her reaction and his slumped shoulders, I imagined that she didn't approve of his viewing the magazine.

"Joey." I tapped his shoulder and pointed. "She just saw what he was looking at and is giving him hell now."

He laughed heartily. I put the magazine away, and we made small talk the rest of the drive.

WE FOUND THE CLINIC WITHOUT too many difficulties. I was grateful that Joey had driven me because I was unfamiliar with San Francisco. Joey navigated the streets like a pro.

We climbed the two flights of stairs to get to the clinic. Joey was several paces behind me, and he got my attention just prior to me opening the front door to the office.

"Hey, Junior," he said as I turned around. "I just wanted to get one last look at you before we went in."

Snap! Snap! I heard. It was the familiar sound of his digital camera.

Joey looked at me from behind the lens and said, "These are the before pictures."

"Come on, Joey?" I asked. "Really?"

"Relax. I'm just trying to lighten up the mood."

We both laughed.

"Dude, you're going to do yourself shortly." And he just laughed.

We were welcomed by a very lovely receptionist. I was getting to be all too familiar with doctor's offices, paperwork, and the protocol that goes along with everything.

I introduced myself and was immediately inundated with page after page that was to be completed prior to the completion for my appointment. *Medical history, genetics* ... they wanted to know every detail of my life, and a check for six hundred dollars. I looked at Joey and said, "My kids are already costing me money."

Joey laughed as he thumbed through magazines

while I completed the paperwork. Once I completed it all, I waited to be called.

"Mr. Street?" I heard as the door opened to the backroom.

I stood up and said, "I'm right here."

"Please come with me."

I looked back over my shoulder to Joey. He gave me the thumbs up as I went through the doorway. The door closed behind me, and I was alone in the hall with a nurse, a magazine and a cup. I laughed because it sounded like the beginnings of a bad joke.

She handed me the magazine and the cup and pointed over my shoulder to the door at the end of the hall. "When you're finished, return the cup to the lab right over here."

The nerves continued. I stood in the entrance of the room crippled with fear. Right before I entered to door to my private room, the nurse asked me, "Do you have any other questions or concerns?"

I hesitated but plodded forward. "I do have one. I'm sort of embarrassed by it, but here it goes."

The look on her face revealed very little; she was very professional.

"How long should this take?" I cut her off, trying to rephrase my question. "What I mean to say is how long should I be in there for? I really have no idea as to what would be appropriate."

She just smiled and turned away. As she walked down the hall, I heard her say, "Come out in ten minutes."

I was relieved. "Thanks." I shut the door and was

alone. Okay. *Ten minutes. I can get it done in ten minutes.* I opened the magazine and got myself situated.

When I was finished I opened the door and looked at my watch. *Two minutes on the nose.* I smiled. I turned down the hall and brought my sample to the lab. The nurse guided me out to the lobby. She walked me to the door that I exited through. No sooner had I gone through the door than I had heard the familiar click of a camera. Joey was taking pictures again, this time the after pictures.

I laughed as I heard him instruct, "Hold that smile right there." I gave him a big smile, and he took a couple of more photos.

"Why?" I asked. "Why on earth did you feel the need to take these pictures of me?"

As he was putting his camera away, he told me. "Look. I've got both a before and an after picture of you at the bank."

Joey's laughter was the best medicine of the day.

"We'll put these on the web. You'll be famous."

"Great. Just what I need."

With all of the paperwork completed and the deposit in the bank, we laughed the whole ride home.

CHAPTER 16

*I was sure that I was going to see
a lot of those Birkenstocks.*

MY FIRST CHEMOTHERAPY TREATMENT WAS to begin on Monday, June 10th, 2002. Though it might sound strange, I was looking forward to beginning chemo. All of the waiting was killing me.

I felt as if I was in some sort of holding pattern since the operation. The beginning of chemo was going to put me in total control. I was actively taking on the fight and was starting to eradicate and purge this disease from my body.

I brought my parents and my now fiancée, Tiffany, with me. They were the ones who were going to care for me, and they needed to know how to treat me.

THE KAISER SAN RAFAEL OFFICE had three oncologists in their office during my treatments. I was referred or assigned to the care of one Dr. Alan Pryor. Perhaps no more than five minutes had passed since I checked in at the front desk when a nurse poked her head out from a side door.

"Wayne Street, Jr?"

I swung my head toward her, and when we made eye contact with each other, she said, "You can come back now."

I followed the nurse through the door with my entourage in tow.

Following standard operation procedures, I am sure, she said, "Let's get your weight and height."

As a ritual, I removed my shoes even though she insisted that it was not necessary. "I always do," I stated. "It's the one constant for me at all of these appointments. This way I know how much my weight changes from one measurement to the next."

She looked at me as if to say, "Whatever." Then she made one little adjustment with the weights. "Okay. It looks like one eighty-five."

I had a feeling that my weight was going to be an important factor for me during my treatments. I had heard that the chemotherapy would cause a drop in weight; I just didn't have any clue as to how drastically it would change.

She took me to an exam room. "I wanted to go over a few items with you prior to Dr. Pryor coming in."

I laughed when she said that. She glared at me as I laughed. I did not get a good vibe from that glare, which killed the smile on my face. I looked to my parents, my father especially, for some badly needed protection from that nurse. I got nothing.

"Now, Dr. Pryor will exam you and go over various procedures for your treatments—all the good and the bad of chemotherapy."

"There's a good part to chemotherapy?" I asked skeptically. "Like what?"

"It'll keep you alive."

As she turned away to do something, I leaned over towards my father and whispered, "If this cancer won't kill me, she certainly would with that attitude."

My father flashed a little grin the way he always does.

While he would smile at my joke, my mother and fiancée rolled their eyes. My mother looked at Tiffany and said, "I don't know why I put up with him." She just shrugged her shoulders.

"Well, I certainly hope that this cancer doesn't kill me," I joked to the nurse, "for my sake and the sake of humanity."

I got a roll of the eyes from the nurse for that. She liked me; I could tell by then. Folding the chart back over, she got up to exit and said very unenthusiastically, "Dr. Pryor will be with your shortly."

THE NURSE HAD LEFT THE door partially ajar. We waited quietly in a sort of awkward and peaceful silence. People kept walking up and down the hall. Each time I saw a body zoom by, I flinched, thinking that person was Dr. Pryor.

I was familiar with the faces of oncology because this was the same place that I had been getting my Remicade treatments. I didn't know one oncologist from the other though. Doctor number one stopped right outside the door. Thinking it was Dr. Pryor, my heart raced, anxious with anticipation. He wore a buttoned-down, collared shirt; long sleeves, with a pair of dark slacks. His tie completed the professional ensemble.

"Is that Dr. Pryor ?" my mother asked me.

"Nope, I guess not," I said, as the doctor turned away and entered the room directly across the hall. "We have two more chances."

The waiting game continued.

Another doctor passed by. She was a younger lady, perhaps early thirties. *Very nice.* She had blonde, curly hair and blue eyes.

"She could be my doctor."

I smiled at my father. He smiled back. Unfortunately, it was not to be; she went on her way to some other patient oblivious to my presence.

"Junior. You are awful," my mother proclaimed. Laughing, she reached across from her seat and slapped me on my leg.

I just laughed.

Another day, another doctor, I thought. "Mom, Dad. What do you think so far?"

My mother, who was never shy of speaking up, started. "I think that we all need to listen carefully to this doctor." She used her concerned voice with that comment. "I want to know how to care for you if an emergency comes up sometime."

"Oh Mom, there will be no emergency." I made that statement boldly and naively. I had no appreciation for the true effects of chemotherapy. It wouldn't be until weeks later as the treatments began to compound on one another.

Our conversation was interrupted with the rap of the door. "Hello. Hello, Mr. Street? Wayne?"

"Yes, that's me," I exclaimed. "Are you Dr. Pryor?"

"I am indeed."

The four of us exchanged hellos, along with handshakes.

He refocused his attention on me and asked, "So, what can I do for you today?"

I was in disbelief—not at the question per se, rather at the casualness of his tone. Not "What can I do for you?" as in an emergency, but a "What can I do for you?" tone of voice, as if we were buying furniture or a television.

He was dressed in coffee brown-colored slacks, the type that you might catch Peter Brady wearing at the height of the 1970s. He donned the traditional white doctor's smock that covered a well-worn vintage shirt from that era.

"I wanted to take the time today to review your upcoming treatments with you."

I tried to listen; however, I was just transfixed with his Birkenstocks. His hair was a classic salt and pepper. A small mustache rested under his nose. He reminded me of an actor from an Adam Sandler movie. I couldn't think of the name of the guy—just another familiar face in the crowd.

His voice started to drone—"The procedure we will be doing is referred to the BEP cycle"—as he went from Cisplatinum to Etopside, then over the Bleomycin, I began to get lost. That was why I brought three extra sets of ears with me to help decipher all of the information that I knew I was going to be inundated with.

"Your chemotherapy will be three cycles, possibly a fourth if we must."

"Excuse me! You said cycle?"

"That is correct. Starting today, you will receive all three drugs for the next five days. It will take about four to five hours per day; then the two succeeding Mondays. Day eight and day fifteen of the cycle, you will get a shot of Bleomycin."

"So each cycle is three weeks?"

"Yes. Then we will start again."

I took all of that in for what seemed like many minutes—in reality, probably only a few seconds or so. "We are really looking at nine weeks of chemotherapy then?"

"Ideally." He paused, using a silly hand gesture—a rolling of the hands that showed that he was leading into something else. "In some instances, we will do a fourth cycle. There could also be some complications that will lead to delays."

"Complications?" my mother interjected.

Our attention turned to her.

"I don't do complications, Doctor," she told him boldly.

"Well, you may not, Mrs. Street. Unfortunately for you and your son, sometimes the cancer does."

That leaves no room for her on that line of discussion. I stole a quick look at my father, who merely shrugged his shoulders.

"I don't want to give you folks any undue stress or worries." He looked back to me, continuing. "Each and every one of us will react differently to treatments. In many cases, there will be no complications. But your Crohn's disease could be a problem. We might have to be prepared for a few extra complications along the way." He continued, "Mr. Street, I'm concerned about potential complications with your Crohn's."

I had accumulated a list of questions to ask him. And by the end of the consultation, I was convinced that he knew his stuff. Through his explanation, he had answered every question on my list.

I nodded. "I know my immune system is already compromised from the Crohn's. Will that be an issue with the chemo?"

"It shouldn't be, but it could be," he replied. "We'll deal with them as they arise though. Do you have any other questions?"

I felt empowered with the information that I had gathered on my own about the treatments, and was put that much more at ease with what he had to add. "No I don't. I think you addressed all of my concerns."

We all shook our heads. "Well, the nurses will be with you shortly to get the chemo going," he said. We thanked Dr. Pryor as he exited. I looked at my parents while holding Tiffany's hand. All we could do was take a deep breath and think, *Wow!*

MINUTES LATER, MY FAVORITE ONCOLOGY nurse, Ruth Ann, came into the room. Ruth Ann was a larger than life woman with a dominating personality. Her smile always put me at ease.

"Welcome to Club Chemo, Junior." In tow with Ruth Ann was one other nurse with all of the tools to get the job done. "Are we ready to rock 'n' roll?"

"Bring it on," I said confidently. I hadn't a clue of what was to come.

I watched intently as she pulled out the needle and prepped my left arm to find a vein that looked "nice and juicy," as she stated, she was ready to stick me. "Here it comes." I tightened up, waiting for the tremendous pain. I felt a little pinch and then it was over.

Ruth Ann hung a hydration pack on the hook, and then pressed the start button on the pump. "Every day, you are going to get a liter of fluids to get you hydrated. What you are going to find is that the chemo is going to dehydrate you. You will get cotton mouth and dryness inside, among other side effects."

The side effects were plentiful, weight loss, hair loss, changes in complexion, and loss of coloring. And those were only the visible effects. Beneath the surface, on a microbiological level, these chemicals were going to wreak havoc on my insides. Chemotherapy doesn't differentiate between red blood cells and cancer cells. As the old cliché goes, "What is the chemo going to kill first—you or the cancer?"

She pulled up the stool and moved toward me.

"You will have to take this pill called Zofran." I took the pill, and with a quick swig of water, the drugs began.

"This drug will help you fight your nausea. You will want to take this each morning and every evening"— she paused—"even if you don't feel any nausea."

"Why does he need to do that?" my mother had interjected.

Turning to face my mother, Ruth Ann said, "Because once the nausea gets started, it usually will not stop. It just kind of digs into your stomach."

As she described that, I envisioned something evil using a sharp tool like a garden trowel carving up my insides. I could feel and imagine the nausea that she was talking about.

"How long might it be before I start feeling any nausea?" I wanted to know.

"You probably won't feel anything for about four to five days." She reached for another bottle as she continued. "But like I said, once you do, it usually will not go away." She opened up another bottle of pills. "Here is a little favorite of mine—Ativan. This should be used when you go to bed. It will help fight the nausea too, and it can be used as a sedative to help you get to sleep at night."

My mother reached out and took the medicine jar into her hand. She glanced over it with the quizzical look that she often gives prior to making a comment of one sort or another.

"Any other questions?" Ruth Ann looked around the room, allowing enough waiting time before moving forward. "I'm going to let the fluids drip and then I'll be back to start the chemo."

I smiled at her and said, "Won't all that fluid cause me to pee like a racehorse though?" I asked.

Mom gave me a dirty look, and Dad laughed a bit.

Ruth Ann just took it all in stride. "Of course it will, honey. The bathroom is just around the corner. Use it as often as you wish."

My comments didn't seem to phase her one bit. I knew this was going to be a little more tolerable with quick-witted comments from her.

"We are in business." She adjusted the bags of fluids as she rose from her stool. "Everything looks good, Junior. I will be back soon."

The four of us sat in silence for the next few minutes. When Ruth Ann came back I asked, "How long will all of this take today?"

As she put up the first bag of drugs, she replied, "About five hours." She glanced at her watch, "It wouldn't be a bad idea if you folks went out and got lunch or do whatever else you might need to do while we're giving Junior his drugs."

My parents packed up and left, but Tiffany stayed with me all day. As we held hands, we sat together quietly. I just went back and forth watching her, the clock, and the drugs drip into my system.

THERE WERE ONLY THREE TRUTHS I learned that afternoon. One: I was scared. Two: as I stared at that drip pole, I realized that I was going to be tethered to it for the next three months. And three: I was sure that I was going to see a lot of those Birkenstocks.

CHAPTER 17

*You might as well hang a sign around
my neck that says I have cancer.*

I'D HEARD OF THE MANY horrors of chemotherapy and seen people suffering from its effect on television. But I'd never been close to anyone, who actually had gone through the day-to-day sufferings of cancer and chemotherapy.

Even though I was informed of all the possible side effects, I didn't fully understand the enormity of them. To be quite honest, I didn't think much of the potential dangers of chemo.

Each day was the same: the agony of the needle stick, followed by two liters of fluids and a lot of peeing, then five hours of the heavy hitting drugs.

Dr. Pryor had told me, "We will drag you through the mud a little bit along the way." *Great, I only hope that they pull me out too.*

Someone came with me each day to keep my company. The first day, it was Tiffany. The second day, it was my mother. Many of my friends and family were volunteering to take a turn because I don't think anyone wanted me to be alone. I did a lot of reading during my time in the oncology. Each trip took about half a day, so I took off my shoes, covered myself with a blanket, and tried to make the best of a bad situation.

By the end of the week, I began to feel a bit of nausea, but nothing too bad. I faithfully kept taking my Zofran as I was instructed to do. I had spent enough time in the previous seven years with the Crohn's, being nauseated, and I wanted to avoid what I could.

I returned for the second week of chemotherapy. I was in and out in five minutes. Just as they had told me in the previous week, all I was getting was a shot of a drug called Bleomycin. It was "harsh stuff" as one nurse put it, but it was going to do the trick. As the second week progressed, I started to notice subtle changes in my body. I ran my fingers through my hair, and I had a handful of hair before I knew it. It sent chills down my spine. I said to my friend, John, that week, "I think this is the beginning of the hair loss," as I showed him a handful of hair.

My fingers began to tingle, another side effect being the temporary nerve loss in my fingertips. My fingertips tingled all of the time. I had difficulties buttoning my shirt or opening a can of soda, among other small tasks. Then there were the burns. The top side of my hands began to blister. The nurse told me those were called "chemo burns." The drugs were actually burning through my skin. I had read about this in Lance Armstrong's book but hadn't believed him. But I was a believer when I felt them blistering up my own body.

I KEPT MY HAIR AS long as I could. As the days progressed, I couldn't put off the inevitable hair loss any longer. Two and a half weeks into chemo, I was pulling out clumps of hair at a time, which left bald patches all over my head. It looked unhealthy. So I called the salon for an appointment to get my hair cut. I'd gone to Dina for several years. She was Joey's older sister. When the receptionist picked up, I asked, "Can I come in and get a haircut this afternoon from Dina?"

She replied, "I'm sorry. She doesn't have any more times available today."

Disappointed, I thanked her and hung the phone up. I was going to have to do it all myself.

I didn't want to have to cut it all out myself, so I called up my buddy, Joey. I was hoping that he would be able to give her a call and get me in there. I replayed the conversation between me and the receptionist to him, and he just laughed. "Don't worry, dude. I'll give her a call and then be right over to pick you up."

We arrived at the salon about a half hour after speaking to each other. Joey stood by my side as Dina began her work. She began by combing my hair. Joey quickly laughed as we both saw the look of horror on her face as her comb got caught in my hair. She gave it a tug, and her comb was full of hair. She wasn't going to need to do any cutting; all she had to do was pull.

I leaned forward just in time to gaze at a bald patch that had just appeared in the center of my forehead. It was the result of the comb.

"I'm so sorry, Junior," she stated. I could see her almost about to break down in tears. "I didn't mean to hurt you."

I reassured her. "Dina, it's fine. It doesn't hurt. It just comes out. Let's just get this over with."

She settled down a bit and pulled out the clippers.

"That a girl," I heard Joey cheer.

We all laughed a little.

She started cutting right away. "I'm going to leave a little on top for you," she declared.

"Why?" I asked, looking at her in the mirror.

"It should just fall out the rest of the way on its own."

"Just get rid of it all."

Moments later, I had a cool summer cut. The hair was gone. Anyone who saw me on the street wouldn't have taken the haircut for anything more. As Joey walked outside with me, I looked at my reflection in the store window. I turned to Joey and said, "You might as well hang a sign around my neck that says *I have cancer.*" We laughed and went on our way.

I WAS KNOCKED BACK TO reality a day later. I was tired, nauseated, and grumpy all day. As the early evening approached, I told Tiffany and my parents.

"I'm going to bed early. I've got a headache."

"Okay," Tiffany said. "I'll come check on you a bit later."

"Sure thing." I gave her a kiss and thanked her.

As I laid down at home that night, my headache began to throb. I tried to massage my temples as the pain quickly moved into the *pounding* stage. Anyone who has ever had a decent-size headache can relate to and understand what I mean. I started to get chills. My body shivered uncontrollably. It was happening for no apparent reason. *What's happening? It's a hundred degrees outside, and I'm freezing.*

Tiffany came in about an hour later to check on me.

"Are you feeling all right?"

I shook my head. "I'm just a little cold; that's all." I was starting to sweat at the same time. I wiped my brow, but it was damp again almost immediately.

"Tiffany, I'm all right now," I shivered. "I'm just trying to warm up."

"I know. I just hate that you have to go through this." She started to cry. "I am going to take your temperature." She left to go grab a thermometer.

The heat, headache, and of course, the chemo were getting the best of me that evening. "Open up," she instructed. We waited.

"One-hundred and two degrees; we're going to the emergency room."

"I don't want to go," I protested.

"Yes, we are," she said. "Remember what the nurse said, that if you get a fever you are to go to the ER."

I nodded, knowing she was right. With the help of

my parents, Tiffany loaded me into the car and drove me to the emergency room. Wrapped in a blanket, sweating profusely, and shivering uncontrollably, I sat in the passenger's seat of my car as she drove me to the ER. It was around 10:00 p.m. when I was admitted to the hospital. The nurses immediately put in an IV for fluids and the ER doctor ordered blood tests to check my numbers.

The extra fluids began to help immensely, that and three extra strength Tylenol I was given. It took about an hour for the complete blood count (CBC) blood tests to come back. The tests confirmed what the doctor had been suspecting.

"Your white blood cell count is low." Pointing to the chart, he continued. "It should be in this range of 4.0 to 12.0, but yours has dropped to about 3.5. This is the cause of our problem."

He started to inquire about my chemo cycles. "What cycle are you on?"

I explained that I was done with the first cycle and beginning the new cycle in the morning.

He took copious notes, scribbling into the file folder. He continued. "Well, I'm not going to write orders about the chemo, but I'll have to send this information to Dr. Pryor. I'm willing to bet that he will postpone the start of the second cycle for a week."

"Why? Can't he just give me a lower dosage?" I was asking, almost pleading for him to support my view.

"I'm afraid not. You see, the drugs you have been taking have a cumulative effect." Pausing, he said,

"That means you will get some drugs on the first day of the cycle, but the effects of them will not reveal themselves to you until, say, the seventh to tenth day."

He looked at me and could tell that I was still not satisfied with his explanation. He continued. "So we need to give your body plenty of rest between treatments. This will, in turn, allow your body's white blood cells, along with other counts, an opportunity to regenerate so that they can help support your body ward off any potential infections that might occur along the way."

"Great," I exclaimed. "I suppose this means that everything will be set back a week then. Correct?"

"Most likely," he stated. "Don't fret over this. It'll all work itself out. There will be no need to keep you overnight. I ordered the nurse to give you one more bag of fluids here." He tapped on the IV bag above my left shoulder. "Then we will check you out. I'll forward everything up to chemotherapy so that Dr. Pryor will be up to speed upon your arrival tomorrow morning."

I thanked the doctor as he exited behind the curtain. A feeling of defeat came over me. *Okay. Just a minor setback,* I concluded. "Tiffany, how're you doing?" I asked.

She had been a trooper. I could see the tiredness in her eyes. There was no need for her to be here this late. She would probably end up staying awake for another three or four hours—waiting for us to be leaving the hospital, then the drive home, and just getting settled back into bed.

"I'm fine," she said, holding back a yawn. "Just

a little tired. Don't worry. We'll get you home really soon."

I was wheeled out to our car by one of the night orderlies around midnight. We'd been at the emergency room for several hours. I looked up into the sky, hoping for a little help from God perhaps. A shooting star darted across the sky from east to west. I made a wish, praying that this would all go away really soon.

CHAPTER 18

*My mortality was becoming
more and more evident.*

TIFFANY AND I ARRIVED EARLY the next morning for my second cycle of chemotherapy. As I entered the building I headed to the stairwell, I looked back at Tiffany. "I'll see you at the top." I had made it a point to take the stairs in lieu of the elevator on my chemo days. By the time I reached the fifth floor I was exhausted. I sat on the top step to take a momentary break. *Wow! This is a little more difficult than I thought.* I heard the door open from above; it was Tiffany. She didn't say anything, but she reached down to help me. As we took our seats in the waiting room, I had an epiphany. My mortality was becoming more and more evident.

I reached out and took her hand. We made eye contact, and I gave her a wink to tell her that everything was going to be all right. She started to flip through her magazine as we waited—*Modern Bride,* or was it *Vogue,* something that didn't strike my attention except for maybe the hot chick on the front cover.

The door opened, and we were greeted by Ruth Ann. "How are you, darlin'?" she asked as she escorted us to my room for the day.

Tiffany stepped right up to fill in Ruth Ann. "We were in the emergency room last night for about three hours." She continued to speak for the next ten minutes more or less. I lay slumped in the chair with my eyes closed as the two of them talked.

As Tiffany finished, Ruth Ann took a seat on the doctor's little green stool. "Sounds like you had quite the night, Junior."

I only nodded.

"I'm going to start this IV and put some fluids in you. Then I'm going to get Dr. Pryor and let him decide what to do with you today."

"Do you think we will get this cycle started though today?" I was practically pleading. I didn't want the chemo put off a week.

"It is doubtful, but I am going to leave that up to him." She then said, "Here is the little pinch." I flinched as per my usual. "It is in, and there are the fluids."

Minutes later, Ruth Ann returned with another bag. "Dr. Pryor will be a few minutes."

While we were waiting for Dr. Pryor, I must've fallen asleep because I was awakened by a tug at my shoe. At the foot of the bed was Dr. Pryor, with chart in hand, glasses on, and looking ready for business. "Good morning. I understand that you hit a bit of a rough patch, Junior."

"It was awful, Doctor." I sat up a bit so that I could speak to him face-to-face. He said that Ruth Ann had filled him in on the ordeal from the previous evening.

He reached out and held my hand. "You know, Junior, it isn't uncommon for patients in your circumstances to experience these types of setbacks in their treatments." He reached for his stethoscope and continued. "Let me check you out here."

He gestured for me to sit up a bit farther. It was a labored effort on my part.

"Take a deep breath in."

I inhaled slowly and then exhaled upon his order. He moved the stethoscope to another location on my back, and the process was repeated.

As he listened, he grabbed my wrist for my pulse. "Your pulse is a little high, and your blood pressure is a bit low for us today." He recorded the data. "I have reviewed your blood counts from last night's CBC tests. Your white count is too low for us to safely move forward with the next chemo cycle. We're going to have to postpone your cycle until next week."

Pulling out a prescription pad, he explained, "The low white cell count makes you vulnerable to potential illnesses that your body would normally fend off when healthy. We're going to give you a drug called Neupogen."

"What'll it do for me?"

"The goal of Neupogen is to assist you in the production of your white blood cells. By next week, your immune system will be up to an appropriate level for us to move forward."

"Excellent, doctor." I sat up to shake his hand.

"Oh by the way, I was doing a bit of research," he said.

"What was it about doctor?"

"Well, in my thirty years of medicine, I have never had someone as young as you with both Crohn's disease and testicular cancer." He pulled out his notepad. "I was intrigued by the circumstances."

Well, slap my butt and call me Charlie. I wish there was some sort of prize for that—preferably a cash prize.

"Do I get a prize or something?" I asked.

"No, no," he said as he shook his head. "I can't help you with that. But I did find a few statistics that might interest you."

"Shoot doctor."

"Well about one in five hundred people get Crohn's by the age of twenty-five, and only about one in eleven thousand will get testicular cancer by the age of twenty-five."

I shrugged my shoulders.

"I don't get it doctor."

I looked blankly at Tiffany. "What does that mean?"

"Well, the chances of you being in your situation are about one in a million," he said. "You are one in a million." He tucked away his notepad, shot us each a smile, and disappeared down the hall.

WE ARRIVED HOME AROUND NOON. It was July fifteenth. The weather was in check with the historical trends: hot,

hot, hot. Dragging myself into the house with my meds, I entered the family room only to sit in the family blue reclining chair.

I sank into it, sinking into a deep sleep. I heard my father come into the room. He covered me with a blanket. It was ninety-five degrees outside, and I was freezing. He exited the room.

My father and Tiffany visited in the living room as I rested in the family room. The sleep was welcomed. Through this whole ordeal, sleep was really the only time I was not in some sort of pain. If I could sleep, I could go without the pain, even if I was one in a million.

CHAPTER 19

*The more miserable I became,
the stronger I was getting.*

AS PER DR. PRYOR'S INSTRUCTIONS with the Neupogen, I was expected to give myself shots, give myself shots for a full week. *No freaking way!* I thought that if I screwed this up, I was going to die.

I racked my brain for nurses that I knew.

There was one that I knew—Karen. I struggled to get to the phone, hoping that I'd be able to get a hold of her. On the other end, I heard the great Texas drawl that I had come to love.

"Hello, Karen. This is Junior."

Immediately, I could hear the concern in her reply.

"Honey, Doug and I have been praying for you each and every night. How're you doing? Is everything going okay?"

I assured her that I was getting by. I needed people like her on my side. I knew that if I was armed with their thoughts and backed with their prayers, I would somehow make it through. Her devotion to God and her faithful prayers are a big part of the reason why I am still here today.

I explained what was happening about the treatments, chemo, the emergency room, and the weeklong setback.

"The truth is I am miserable."

"I'm sure you are, honey."

"This morning, at the doctor's, they told me that I was to take Neupogen for the next week."

Before I could finish my sentence, I think that she had read my mind.

"I can give you those shots if you want. It can be our little secret." *Perfect!*

For five straight days, she came to my house to do the shot for me. After each shot she smiled and patted my stomach saying, "There you go, sweetie. It's all over." I thanked her every day with a hug and a kiss on the cheek.

MY ENERGY CAME BACK SLOWLY with each passing day. The side effects worsened though. By midweek, my hips were causing such discomfort that I could barely walk. The pain was from the increased production of white blood cells in my bones.

I was able to withstand the pain from the hips, but the small of my back throbbed relentlessly. I was even having difficulties sitting still for short periods of time. The more miserable I became, the stronger I was getting. Thanks to Nurse Karen and the shots, I was strong enough to finish the six weeks of chemotherapy.

THE SECOND CYCLE FINISHED RATHER uneventfully. I had been administered the full, five-day regiment of drugs. It was just painful, boring, and arduous. And like the first cycle, the second and third week of the cycle were also done without incident.

In my off time, all I did was sleep, watch television, and rest for the upcoming days of chemo. I waited and hoped that I would be strong enough for the next treatment. I remember what the doctor had told me. "The chemo won't just kill the cancer, but it will kill you too." It was a race of destruction, and I wasn't sure what was going to be completely destroyed first: the cancer or me. I was afraid that it might be a race too close to call.

The third cycle was going to finish off the last of whatever cancer cells were in me. My biggest concern about the third cycle was that it wasn't going to work and that I was going to have to possibly do a fourth cycle. I knew in my heart of hearts that I wasn't going to make it through a fourth cycle.

I RELIED HEAVILY ON ZOFRAN and Ativan every day. These two prescriptions were staples during the ten weeks of chemo. As one nurse told me, "The nausea will be coming, and it will be coming on strong. You gotta take these drugs even when you think you don't need them."

Once it starts, it won't stop. I thought about those words every time I took my pills. Some days, I'd feel fine while other days, I would need help just to get to the bathroom or up around the house.

IT WAS EARLY AUGUST. I'D been in chemo for seven weeks, and it had been ten weeks since I learned I had cancer. My body was just about ready for the third cycle. As we started the cycle, I felt like a football player nursing an injury and sent back onto the field too early. The third cycle would only compound the effects of the previous two cycles.

Ruth Ann came to start my cycle. "Hey Junior, you're looking good. Anything exciting happening these days?"

Nausea, no hair, I thought to myself. *Nothing unusual, this happens to us all.*

"No, I'm fine," I told her. "Will the doctor be in today?"

"He should be here any minute," she replied. She fixed the Etoposide and headed on her way to another patient.

Moments later I heard, "The numbers look good," as I looked up to see Dr. Pryor arrive. "Your tumor markers are down from over twenty-five thousand to about two hundred. We're almost there." They had improved from the previous weeks, thankfully. "How are things going?"

There was a problem with my bladder. "I've been peeing blood."

"Really?" I'd piqued his interest. "What's been happening? Can you describe it?"

"I noticed a few days ago that when I urinate, there is blood in it." I paused, trying to find the right word. "It has created an unusual orange tinge to it."

He pulled out his prescription pad. "Here." He handed me a sheet of paper. "Take that to the pharmacy. This medicine will help fight this infection."

I thanked him, and he exited the room.

ONE DAY, TWO DAYS, SEVEN days—still no improvement. The bleeding was becoming worse and more frequent. The next week, I came in for my ten-minute chemo shot and I had my blood drawn. My numbers had receded, therefore weakening my immune system. My energy and strength had receded too.

Ruth Ann came in to report the lab results. "Junior, you're pretty weak today." She set an IV for my fluids. "Dr. Pryor has ordered a blood transfusion."

"What for?" I asked. "How can this help?"

"This blood transfusion will perk you right up, Junior," the nurse reassured me. "It will help your immune system. Unfortunately, I'll have to stick you with a bigger needle though because the blood is thicker."

"Interesting. I thought that was just an expression." I flinched as she stuck me with the needle.

She shook her head. "No, darling. It's true."

MY TEN-MINUTE TRIP TO CHEMO took three hours because of the blood transfusion. Ruth Ann had been right. I started to feel a bit better right away. I just hoped it would last. As I waited patiently for the blood to drip through the IV and into my veins, my mind wandered. I thought of my friends out that week at Lake Trinity for our annual camping trip. It was the first one I had missed in the seven years we went camping. *Ah, camping in the woods. What a nice retreat from this crap.* I needed a break, and that would've been a great outlet for me. *How fun and relaxing that would be.* I was getting excited. When the nurse came in, I told her about our trip. "Doesn't that sound like fun, Ruth Ann?"

"Honey, sure it does." She looked me up and down and told me, "But you are in no shape to go camping. If you question me, I will stick the doctor on you too." She pointed her finger at me, and she meant it. I could tell.

I faded away into sleep shortly after that. I was awakened about two hours later, exhausted, nauseated, and groggy.

"All done, Junior. You can go home now. See you next week for your last shot."

I thanked her, and as I dragged my butt down the stairs to my car, I just laughed at myself. *I wanted to go camping.* Ha!

CHAPTER 20

Crap. I could have done without that.

NINE WEEKS OF CHEMOTHERAPY HAD left me bald, nauseous, pale, and dehydrated. The dehydration led to general fatigue and a nagging headache. I was hydrating with glass upon glass of water.

The more water I drank, the more I had to pee. The more I urinated, the more I bled, and the more I hurt.

The week dragged on. I was marching toward my last treatment of Bleomycin. It was Thursday evening when I pulled out the calendar. *Four days to go.* It was the weakest I had ever felt. My mother was at the Giants' game with my siblings. My father and Tiffany were tending to me that evening. My father adjusted my blanket over my toes as Tiffany served me a cup of soup. As I sipped from the mug, I thought of the hot soup on that hot August night. It didn't seem right. I had to smile at that thought because nothing really did seem right to me anymore.

I was asleep before the sun went down. Awaking around ten that evening, I had to pee. The nausea persisted.

The room was spinning around me. I was light-headed. As I stood up, it took me several seconds to gather my equilibrium as I shifted from side to side. I mustered the strength to go to the bathroom. All the lights were off; everyone must've been asleep.

As I stood there in the bathroom, I had to hold my hand out against the bathroom wall to support myself. *What is happening to me?* I began to panic. I finished, washed my hands, and made my way back to the kitchen.

My father had come downstairs. He stood in the kitchen looking at me. "I heard a noise. Is everything all right, Junior?"

"I'm not sure, Dad," I replied as I rested against the kitchen countertop. "I need a glass of water."

He hurried over and told me, "Sit down on the couch, and I'll get you a glass."

I nodded in approval. All along, I had to lean on something to maintain my balance.

Dad walked over toward me. "Here you are. Do you need anything else?"

"Thanks," I said as I tried to adjust myself in my seat. "I'll be all right." I took one more big gulp of water before I headed back to bed.

"I think I'm going to stay down here a bit longer."

He sat down on the couch and flipped on the news. "Good night, Junior."

It must have been around two in the morning when I wrestled myself out of bed, once again, courtesy of my full bladder.

I felt worse than I had the previous time. *Should I go to the emergency room?* I shook off that thought. I didn't want to pay the fifty dollars for the ER visit. I decided that I would go to the ER in the morning if the situation didn't seem to progress, then at least I could get my mother to pay for it.

As I walked down the three steps to get to the bathroom, I took a tumble. Nothing was hurt, except a bit of my self-esteem. *Crap. I could have done without that.*

It was a long ways up from the floor. I eventually made it into the bathroom. I peed with pain as the blood from my bladder rushed into the toilet bowl. The room began to spin again. I envisioned myself passing out right on the spot, hitting my head on the porcelain bowl, only to be found in the morning once the rest of the house had risen.

That was not to be. I made it out of the bathroom; however, my body felt heavier; there was an entirely new problem.

I ran through a list in my head. *Upset stomach; no hair; weight loss; bleeding; bladder infection; and, great, now this.* I couldn't believe what was happening as I studied my joints. I was beginning to experience an inordinate amount of swelling in my joints. I could barely bend my arms and legs because of all the swelling.

I COULDN'T GET BACK ALL the way to my bedroom, so I stopped at the couch.

As the first light arrived, my mother had come rumbling down stairs. Another sibling of mine was up and about. The house was coming alive by the minute while I seemed to be fading away by the second.

"Mom." I waved her over. "I need your help."

She looked me up and down. "What can I get you?" She glanced over the kitchen counter to me on the couch.

"I think I need to go to the emergency room."

"We'll get Tiffany up, and she can take you."

My mother went into the bedroom to get her up. Tiffany had slept straight through the night, uninterrupted by my trips to the bathroom. She had the uncanny ability to sleep through just about anything. It was amazing. She could sleep through a herd of elephants.

Within thirty minutes, she and I were in the car.

"Call me when you get him checked in," I heard my mother shout to Tiffany as we drove away.

I was nearly immobile by this time. I couldn't find a comfortable position in the passenger's seat. It was only a twenty-minute drive. It wasn't coming soon enough. She kept rubbing my shoulder as she drove. "It'll be okay, Junior."

I only nodded to acknowledge that I heard what she had said.

She pulled right up to the front of the ER, parking in the handicap spot. She walked around to the passenger side to help me out of the car. I waived her off.

"Please just go inside and get some help."

I watched as she stormed through the double doors and almost instantly came out followed behind by two orderlies in their white uniforms, one of whom was pushing a wheelchair. Together, they lifted me out of the car and into the wheelchair.

Months later, I recall Tiffany making a comment later on to the effect of, "I knew that he was in bad shape when he couldn't walk into the ER." She knew that I was a proud and determined individual. It was unlike me to ask for such assistance as a wheelchair.

I was immediately taken back to a room and hooked up to an IV. I didn't understand the full gravity of the situation at the time as the nurses hustled around me.

WITH TIFFANY'S HELP, WE FILLED the doctor in on the previous evening's struggles. They were going to test for the cause of my bladder infection. The first test was to have me pee in a cup. I had no luck; it's hard to pee on demand.

They also drew blood. It was vital to determine the status of my immune system. The doctor wanted to get my white blood cell count and red blood cell count. If there was an infection running rampant in my body, then I was going to need a strong immune system to be prepared to fight this off.

The doctor fired question after question at me. "How long have you had this bladder problem?"

I softly said, "About two weeks." I pointed to my

bag that I had brought. Tiffany pulled out a bottle of pills. "This is what Dr. Pryor prescribed for me."

"Has it been working?" he asked.

"No. Every day has just seemed to be worse."

"Well, as soon as we get those tests back, we will be able to treat you."

He flipped over the chart. "We are going to keep you overnight."

"Overnight?" I protested. "It is only eight in the morning. Can't we see how I'm doing later this afternoon?"

"You're in no shape to argue with me," he told me.

"We've got a wedding to go to tomorrow afternoon," I said. "Will I be able to go to that?"

He shook his head. "You won't be going anywhere anytime soon." He continued. "I'll be back to see you in a while. Until you pee in this cup, keep sucking down those fluids." He pointed to the drip bag.

That must be doctor humor. *Suck down those fluids.*

He shut the curtain behind him as he exited. Tiffany sat down by my bedside.

"This sucks," I declared.

"I know, honey." She reached into her purse. "I brought a magazine. Do you want to look at it with me?"

I had nothing else to do. "Sure. What is it about?"

"It's a bridal magazine. Let me tell you a few ideas I had about our wedding." She began to flip the pages. I could see the glow in her face. She was looking beyond the currently bad situation. She was ready for our wedding. I wish I could've shared her optimism.

Unfortunately, a wedding was the furthest thing from my mind. My joints throbbed. She talked, and I nodded from time to time. Occasionally, she would ask me what I thought. I would try to defer to her by saying something like, "You should pick. You have good taste. What do you like?"

I WAS NOT AS ACTIVE of a participant as I could have been and most definitely should have been. If I could go back and do it all over again, I would have delved into the planning right along with her. After all, it was *our* wedding, not hers.

I had proposed about eight weeks earlier. I had dragged my feet long enough, but I knew I couldn't hold out forever. Tiffany had been the best thing that ever happened to me. I would've been crazy to let her slip away because of my reluctance.

I could spin you a tail and talk about the roses, the candle lit dinner, the music, or the sunset, that were all part of the perfect proposal. Regrettably I had proposed under less romantic circumstances.

I had bought a ring several months before the cancer and tucked it away in my pocket. I was biding my time for the perfect moment. Needless to say, the cancer caught us both off guard. So one afternoon when we were driving home from a hospital visit and stopped at a red light I pulled the ring out of my pocket and casually handed the ring to her. "Hey, you want to marry me?" I asked. The rest was history.

As unflattering as it might have been, it still is a memorable moment that we both laugh at.

WE TALKED FOR ABOUT TWO hours after we met with the doctor in the emergency room. I was finally beginning to stabilize. I still hadn't been able to pee in the container for them either. There was just something about someone asking you to pee that was a real turn off. After a couple of tries, I was able to give them the sample they wanted.

While Tiffany and I waited for the tests to come back that morning, I was given several more drip bags. I must've had a hundred liters of fluid dripped into me over the succeeding hours. In reality, it was probably just two or three. I was peeing it out just as fast as the fluids were dripping into me. And it wasn't any less painful. It felt as if I was pissing glass.

By four that afternoon, I was ready to check out and go home. I asked Tiffany, "Will you get my stuff so that I can put my shorts on?"

She replied quietly by saying, "Why don't we just wait a couple more minutes for the nurse or doctor to come by."

At her request I waited reluctantly. I settled into the bed and tried to relax. I was in pain and I asked Tiffany, "Do you think they can get me something for my pain?" I was thinking about ibuprofen but hoping for something a little bit strong like Vicodin or even morphine.

Tiffany went to go fetch a nurse. She reappeared

moments later with two nurses. "Hey there, honey," the nurse said. "We're going to take you up to the fifth floor."

As she and her co-worker began to unlock the bed, I began to panic. "The fifth floor? I was not going to stay overnight. I thought that I'd made that clear?"

"Oh, sure you will, Junior." I watched as she pulled out a needle. "Here is a little bit of medication that will help to ease the pain. You won't even know what—"

I never heard her finish her thought.

It must have been an hour or two later that I came to. When I awoke, I saw tiffany thumbing through her *Bride* magazine with my mother. My father sat watching the television.

"Hey, Junior. You were out for quite a while. How are you feeling?"

Miserable, I told myself. "I think I'm feeling a little better." I glanced around the room. *At least I have a private room,* I thought. "Where are we?"

"Don't you remember? The nurse brought you to your own room about two hours ago."

I was rubbing my eyes and trying to sit up. "I don't recall any of it." My groin was on fire.

Tiffany stood up. "I'm going to go get a nurse. They told me to once you were up again."

"Sure thing," I said as I watched her scurry out of the room. "I'll just be right here." I looked around and I smiled at my parents. I guess they had arrived while I was out.

My mother stood up to stand at my bedside.

"Hey, Mom." I reached for her hand. "How was your day?"

"It was okay. I spent a little time getting ready for school."

We were interrupted as Tiffany came back in with a doctor.

"Hello, Junior. I'm Dr. Forrester. I'll be treating you tonight." He flipped open my chart and took a seat at the foot of my bed. He stood about six foot three and was a dark, handsome man. He had a George Clooney look to him. "We've gotten your test results back. You're in some pretty bad shape."

"What tipped you off?"

"I've got some good news for you. We've identified the problem. You have a bladder infection. We're going to treat it with a series of antibiotics." He pointed up to the IV pole.

I noticed that there was not just one but four different bags of fluids hanging above my head.

"So, when can I go home?" I really just wanted him to cut to the chase.

"That is the bad news." He reached for the television remote. He turned the television on to channel four. "You are under strict orders to watch football and relax." He adjusted the volume for me and handed me the remote. "You won't be going anywhere tonight," he declared. "Do you have any questions?"

"Yes, Doctor." I pulled down the covers and lifted up my gown. "What can you do about this swelling? It is so painful."

I watched as my father turned away. My mother, Tiffany, and the doctor all stared.

"I read in the report that you had been experiencing some swelling." He paused. "I've got to be honest though; I hadn't quite anticipated this."

I watched as he put a latex glove on to examine me.

"It started in the middle of last night and just kept getting bigger and bigger." I repositioned myself in the bed, in obvious discomfort.

I watched his eyes the entire time. "This is a form of edema swelling."

"What does that mean?" I asked. "This isn't normal, is it?"

"Swelling is a normal result of the chemo," he said, pointing at me, "but this type of swelling is a bit much. I've never seen it before."

"A bit much?" I raised my voice. "I've never seen a melon this big, let alone my scrotum."

"The swelling is going to have to run its own course. It may be a day. It may be a couple of months."

"A couple of months?" I was in disbelief. "It hurts so much."

"Junior, we'll do everything we can to take care of this problem for you."

I just shook my hand. "You have to be kidding me." I could feel myself getting wound up and losing what little strength that I had remaining. Once again, I felt defeated. "Well, it hurts to get up and go to the bathroom. All of the extra weight is killing me."

"I'll send a nurse into the room in a few minutes to administer you with some morphine." He closed up the chart and reassured me that everything was going to be all right.

AFTER DR. FORRESTER LEFT, MY scrotum continued to swell. It was becoming engorged. The pain was the worst of my entire life, bar none. I didn't know anything on my body could get *that big*. The nurse attending to me that first night in the hospital was a dude. I'm sure that I got his name at some point; maybe it was Joe, or perhaps it could have been Bill. I just called him Focker, after the Ben Stiller character in the movie *Meet the Parents*.

I was becoming delusional. My condition was getting worse. I was calling out for Focker pretty frequently and asking for drugs that would help to ease the pain.

Focker held up the needle. "I have some right here. I was going to start you off with two milligrams and see how you do."

Two? Two milligrams? I thought to myself that he had to be joking. "There is more than two milligrams in there." I pointed to the syringe. "Give it all to me."

He opened up an alcohol swab to clean off the entry to the IV line. He then injected the needle into the tube and shot me up with my first morphine. *Ahh.* I smiled in relief. *Amazing,* I thought to myself. *It works so quickly.*

After he had given me that first shot, he told me, "You will feel a big change right away."

I thanked him.

He nodded and exited the room. It was late. My parents said their good-byes for the night. I told Tiffany that she better head home too so she could get some rest for our friend's wedding the next day. She told me that she was staying with me a little bit longer.

She sat there with me as we watched football. It was the Eagles and the Bears in a preseason game. *Oh the suffering.* We conversed with some sparse conversation from moment to moment. I faded in and out with the help of the morphine. I felt Tiffany give me a kiss on the cheek before she left for home.

Focker returned every two hours to keep me drugged.

THE NEXT MORNING BEGAN WHEN one of the nurses woke me up around six in the morning so that she could draw "a little blood." I learned quickly that my days in the hospital were not going to be twenty-four hour days. Here, they were going to be eight hours. That is the length of the shifts for the nurses.

Around six each morning, one nurse would come into check my vitals. This was a standard routine, as I could recall, for them to wrap up their shift. No sooner would I get to go back and close my eyes than would the new nurse come into start her shift by checking the same vitals (blood pressure, pulse, etc.). It isn't difficult to believe that I was to get more and more agitated as I was getting continually disrupted.

AROUND MIDMORNING THE FOLLOWING DAY, Tiffany and my mother had returned to spend time with me. The nurses had made their rounds. They fed me, they bled me, and they drugged me. It was all part of a strict regime that was supposed to heal me. I was keeping my fingers crossed.

My groin was so big I couldn't get out of bed any more to urinate. At the urging of the doctor, a nurse inserted a catheter. If you don't know what one is, you can Google it.

At one point—though I couldn't recall when—a team of nurses entered my room, along with a doctor. It was now late morning. The weekend staff was in control of the hospital.

"Ladies, we need you to pack up all of your stuff," ordered the doctor.

"Is there any sort of problem?" my mother asked.

"We're moving Junior down to ICU. We need to monitor him a bit more closely." That was all he said.

I wasn't in any position to speak. I had just gotten my morphine for breakfast, and my world was spinning as the nurses twirled my bed around and roll me to another part of the hospital.

"Wee!" I shouted as I was sped down the hall.

When the nurses got me settled into the ICU, a doctor came in and began to tell me some of the protocol of the intensive care. "Junior, with your immune system compromised, we will have to keep you in this environment for a few days."

I struggled to sit upright. "A few days?" I shook my head in disapproval. "We have a wedding to go to this afternoon." I was pointing back and forth with my hand between myself and Tiffany.

"I'm sorry to ruin your plans, Junior."

He meant business; I could tell.

"You won't be going anywhere."

I was crushed. *What would Mike say?* I didn't have his contact information, so I couldn't let him know that I wasn't going to be able to make it.

As my mother got ready to leave for the day, she made sure that I was getting situated properly. "Is there anything I can do for you, honey, before we leave?"

I had to get a hold of Mike, I had kept telling myself. "Would you please call Coach Derkos for me?" I couldn't just stand my friend up and I knew that Coach would be attending the wedding. I figured the least I could do was relay a message through him.

My mother agreed to do so. "What do you want me to tell him?"

"He is going to be at Mike's wedding. You need to tell him that we won't be attending the wedding and that I am stuck here in the hospital."

She was writing down the important parts of the message for me.

She promised me that she would get this done. Moments later, Tiffany and my mother both left the ICU to go about their days. The only options I had for the day were three channels of television, a fantasy football magazine, sleep, and discomfort.

AS THE DAY PROGRESSED, MY health was digressing. I was feeling nauseated, and there was increased swelling. The nurse came in, and she chatted with me a bit. "Junior, how're you feeling?"

At that point, I was on the constant verge of tears.

With my eyes welling up, I shivered uncontrollably. The nurse stepped forward to give me a shot of morphine. I was shaking in anticipation. I was feeling like an addict. I needed the drug and wanted it right then and there. Once the shot was administered, I could feel the calm come over my body once again.

My groin wasn't getting any better though. I saw the nurse pull back the covers to look at my groin and say, "Well, my goodness, dear. I can't imagine that that is any comfort to you," as she shook her head. She pulled something out from her pockets as she was speaking to me. When she stretched it out between her hands, I realized that she had a tape measure in her hand, the type that a woman (I suppose any person) would use when sewing. "Let's just has a quick look and see how big your swelling has gotten to be now."

I just sort of shrugged as I realized it was almost too comical. Despite the pain, this was nearly too humorous. She adjusted my important parts so that she could, in her own words, "Lets get an accurate measurement." She then declared, "Your scrotum is now over_____ inches in diameter."

She put her tape measure away and continued. "If there is anything else that you might need, just ring the bell. I'll be back to check in on you a little later on."

EARLY THAT EVENING, MY FATHER arrived at the hospital after he had returned from church. I was suffering from uncontrollable shaking, more like tremors. I couldn't get warmed up. With my blood pressure dropping and pulse rising, the doctor on call ordered a blood transfusion.

A new nurse came into the room. He looked more like a hippie than a nurse to me—a bushy beard with a ponytail, though he had a great bedside manner. He was in the room with Nurse Suzie, my father, and probably someone else. He was a powerful person, grabbing control of the situation and reassuring me and the family that things were going to start getting better.

"This transfusion"—he paused as he was hanging the sack on the IV pole before he continued—"will perk you right up by boosting your blood counts. Right now, your body is working extremely hard and needs a little pick-me-up so to speak. I got the juice right here for you." He tapped on the bag twice and smiled as he stuck me in my left forearm to get the new IV started.

I continued to shake.

My body was under major duress, dizzy, weak, and hot while fading in and out of consciousness. I was running a fever of 103, sweating profusely, and freezing all at the same time.

I had heard the doctor whisper to a nurse, "His body is beginning to shut down." My immune system was severely compromised from the ten weeks of chemotherapy. My white blood cell count was down to 0.1. For all practical purposes, I had no white blood cells. I had no immune system.

I felt like I was part of a science experiment. Lying in my hospital bed, the nurses had five different monitors collectively running. One on my chest; others were carefully placed at different key pulse points on my body. Three nurses entered the room. Focker sat down near my bedside.

He pulled out a needle. "Well, Junior, just sit back and relax. This work we are doing will get you feeling better real soon. I promise." He spoke in a calming voice. I felt reassured and confident when he spoke.

"Okay." I was shivering, and my teeth were chattering as I spoke.

"You are getting a bit dehydrated, so we are going to run a second IV for you."

I felt a prick in my left arm.

"Breathe, honey," I heard from another nurse. She reached for my hand. I could feel the latex gloves against my skin. "Deep breath in."

Following her instructions, I labored to fill my lungs.

"Good, sweetie. Good. Now a deep breath out."

I exhaled.

My mind was fading toward unconsciousness. I glanced at the faces in the room, two nurses, a doctor, my father, and Tiffany. They were all wearing masks over their faces. I rolled over to the side, and I glanced at the monitor that read all of my vital signs.

"What is happening to me?"

Focker spoke up. "We are charting your oxygen levels, blood pressure, and pulse rate."

"Well, how am I doing?" I asked.

He hesitated.

Not good, was what I was reading from his face.

"You're doing great Junior, just keep breathing." He walked away and I watched him whisper something to my parents. I learned later that everyone around me knew the end was near. My parents and fiancée had been told by the doctors that everything that could be done was, in fact, done.

"All we can do is wait and pray," my mother recalled the doctor saying that night.

Focker came back over to me and explained my vitals to me. "Your blood pressure is low at ninety over forty."

A person my age should have a blood pressure more upwards of 120 over 80.

"Your pulse is at ninety-two beats per minute."

I knew the average resting heart rates should be about sixty beats per minute. My resting pulse was typically around forty-five beats per minute. My heart was working overtime and not getting any blood pumped. It is amazing how quickly your body can turn on you.

My oxygen level in my blood was also being measured. "Your oxygen level is at 85 percent. That is why you are so lightheaded at the moment."

"Where should my oxygen level be?" I recall asking.

"We like to see it at least at 90 percent." The nurse motioned to the monitor. "A healthy person will have it normally at 95 percent."

I KNEW THAT I WAS losing the battle. The cancer was all but gone; the most recent blood test had told me that. Unfortunately my immune system was nonexistent. I had nearly won my battle against cancer but I was about to die from a routine infection. *Oh, the irony.*

Only two people could be in the room with me at a time. No one with even the slightest hint of a cold could be around me. A simple cold could have done me in too. So that was why everyone wore masks. My parents, Tiffany, younger sister and twin brothers took turn sitting with me.

That night my younger brother, Bobby, phoned the emergency room. He was in Missouri visiting some friends.

"Don't you die," he demanded. "Don't you go away on me."

I smiled and just chuckled.

I TRIED TO PASS THE time that night by counting the blood drops dripping through the tubes. As I watched the blood drip, it seemed a type of Chinese water drip torture. Drip after drip, one drop at a time. For all practical purposes, watching the transfusion take place was similar to watching grass grow. It wasn't happening.

As the night wore on, and the blood dripped, the tears flowed as my parents, family members and medical personal streamed in and out of my room.

Everyone held hands as I lapsed in and out of delirium. A priest arrived to read me my last rites.

"Amen," I heard. The circle around me broke up as the nurse came back in.

"Excuse me, everyone," she said as she approached my parents. "We need to ask a couple of you to leave. We can only have two people visiting at a time."

The priest, my brothers, and Tiffany left. The nurse said, "We need one more."

"But there are only two of us left."

"Oh, but Junior's uncle just arrived and is out in the waiting room. He asked to come in."

I shifted a little bit. I looked over to my father. "Who's here, Dad? Do any of them know I'm here?"

"I don't know, Junior. Let me see."

The glass wall to the room had the curtain drawn. No one could look in, and I certainly couldn't see to the outside. I watched the curtain peel back as my uncle entered.

It was "Uncle Izzy." Izzy Derkos my junior college tennis coach was one of the most influential people in my life. He had taken me in at the junior college and onto his tennis team. He had taught me that if I worked I could hold the world in the palms of my hands.

I'd always viewed him on a pedestal; he was larger than life. At that moment, as he entered the room dressed in a dark gray suit and tie, he was nothing less than angelic.

I immediately started rambling, struggling to sit up in the bed and come to attention for the man. "I'm so sorry, Izzy," I began as tears rolled down my face. I continued. "I'm a mess. I'm so sorry that you have to see me this way."

"No. No, Junior," he interrupted. "Captain Street, you are looking good." He was always so articulate when he spoke had an uncanny ability to put people at ease. His charm, character, and overall persona were absolutely what I need at that moment.

I was still crying as I tried to speak to him. "The doctor says that I cannot shake hands with anyone because of the germs. I wish I could."

He reassured me. "I know you would. Don't worry about it. I just wanted to come by and see my main man tonight."

He looked around the room and walked over to greet my father. Next to my father, he started to talk about Mike's wedding.

"My wife and I were coming home from Mike's wedding."

"How did everything go?"

"It was a beautiful ceremony," he declared. "Of course, it wasn't the same without you there. I did, however, pass along the message to the bride and groom for you."

My crying had subsided and I was able to carry on with him in a somewhat coherent conversation. "How did you get in here? You know they only are supposed to let family in here."

"It was easy." He smiled. "I just explained the situation to the nurse. I might have fibbed and told her I was family. I had to get in here and see my favorite player. I couldn't imagine going home without checking in on you tonight."

We carried on for a few more minutes.

I was embarrassed lying there helplessly in the ICU as he watched. I had always been afraid to disappoint him, in most cases even more so than disappointing my parents. Most of my teammates and fellow alumni would agree with me. I guess I cried because of the disappointment that I thought he saw in me that night. All of the strength and training that I had developed and worked on over the years had been washed away in less than a ten-week period of time because of the cancer.

There wasn't anything that I could do about it, and I imagine that Izzy felt just as helpless. I think we both got what we needed that night.

He gave me the spiritual boost that I needed that night. He had always brought out the best in me and he was witnessing me at my worst. I was bound and determined to get out of that ICU and show him my best once again. It didn't matter how long it took; it just mattered that I did.

As we wrapped up our visit, Izzy stood by my bed.

"Junior, it was good to see you. You look great. I've got to get headed home now. I'll get back in touch with you later in the week. Got that?"

"Yes, sir," I stuttered out as the chills continued.

And like that, he turned and disappeared behind the curtain.

I faded away. The next thing I knew, I opened my eyes and glanced around. I remember asking myself if I was dead or alive. The nurse came in to check my vitals.

"Good morning, Junior."

It was morning. I made it through the night.

CHAPTER 21

I needed nine innings of baseball.

I SPENT EIGHT NIGHTS IN ICU, under round the clock watch. I had stabilized thanks to a blood transfusion, nurses, doctors, and morphine.

As I lay in my hospital bed that twelfth morning, I wanted to go home.

The nurse entered the room and began her morning routine. She asked, "How're you today, Junior?"

When I replied that I was "fine," she noticed that I seemed to be a bit more chipper.

So she said, "You seem to be feeling better. It is good to see that."

"I'm doing great today," I declared. "I want to go home today."

"You do?" She stopped her writing to find out more. "We will just have to get the doctor over here at some point today to check you out and give his clearance."

I shook my head, but before she left, I made one last request. "Nurse, it is about ten right now. I want to be home in time to watch the Oakland A's play tonight."

"I'll see what I can do for you."

I thought, *Excellent. I can't wait.*

I needed to get home for of all things a television with full cable. I'd been stuck watching daytime soap operas and had gone without sports, baseball above all. The Oakland A's were going for their Major League record twentieth win that evening. I'd only been able to follow them in ICU through news clips. I needed more; I needed nine innings of baseball.

TIFFANY HAD ARRIVED IN THE early afternoon, and we sat around in the room. I had had Tiffany go find a nurse every half hour to see if there were any signs of the doctor. Nothing!

She had helped me get out of bed and gingerly go for a brief but needed walk out of my room to pass the time.

When we returned to the room, we still had to wait. Around five thirty that evening, I had officially declared the situation hopeless. There had been no sign of the doctor. I asked the nurse one last time. "Excuse me, Nurse. Do you know if Dr. Forrester will be able to see me tonight and check me out?"

"Junior, we haven't seen him all day." She looked at me. I imagine that she did see the disappointment in my face at that moment. "I'll go call over to his office one last time for you."

"Thanks."

Alas, he arrived shortly after the nurse made her final call. I was so excited I nearly fell out of my bed. He calmed me down and said, "I understand that you're ready to go home right now?"

"Absolutely," I said. "I need to get home by seven p.m. to watch the A's play their baseball game tonight."

"I heard about them. They are on quite a winning streak, aren't they?"

"Yes. They have won the last nineteen games and are going for number twenty tonight."

"Well, let me have you sit up here so that I can check you out."

I did as I was instructed, and he listened to my breathing and heart rate.

It was a routine inspection. He then tucked his stethoscope away and called for a nurse. "Nurse, would you please come in here now?"

A nurse immediately entered into the room promptly. Dr. Forrester directed his attention at her.

"Would you please take that IV out of Junior's arm and get him cleaned up so that he can get home to the ball game tonight?"

"Yes, Doctor." She immediately went to work. I was enthused by the news.

"Thanks, Doctor," I said. "Could you tell me what is next?"

"Well, let me see." He flipped through the chart.

"I will be ready for my fourth round of chemotherapy whenever Dr. Pryor wants to do it."

He looked up from his chart. "We have your last

blood test back." There was a tense hesitation. "The tumor markers are back to normal levels."

"What does that mean?"

He looked at me and then at Tiffany. "There is no more cancer."

The weight of the world had been lifted off my shoulders. Tiffany slid over to hug Dr. Forrester.

He extended his hand to me and said, "Now go home and get better."

A half hour later, I was being pushed in a wheelchair through the lobby of the hospital and out to the parking lot where Tiffany was waiting with the car running. We were headed home to surprise my family. They were expecting Tiffany, but not me.

I'd only been gone twelve days, and it felt like an eternity.

We were headed home.

ME, TIFFANY, AND THE REST of my family enjoyed the game together that evening. In the bottom of the ninth inning, the score was tied eleven to eleven—down to the last strike. With one swing of the bat, Scott Hatteberg hit a solo homerun over the right field wall for the Oakland A's record twentieth win.

We all shared the jubilation as we watched Hatteberg round the bases. We celebrated that night because we all knew that the streak would go on, and so would I.

CHAPTER 22

"It just wasn't your time to go."

—*Steve Stedman,*
teacher, colleague, and friend.

MY RECOVERY WAS A LONG and winding road. The chemotherapy that had saved my life had left my body ravaged. My body was fragile, but my mind was strong. The worst was over and I wasn't sure why, but I had survived. As we headed home, I took comfort in a colleague's words, "It just wasn't your time to go."

I've never had another relapse with the cancer. Life has gone on. And in the years since, I've caught myself reflecting on my life and on the incredible series of events that have brought me to the present: tennis, love, modern medicine and above all fate.

NEARLY EVERYONE IN MY LIFE is connected to me through tennis in one way or another. All of our racquets had crossed paths somewhere at sometime. My best friends are tennis players. One of my closet friends John and I had met playing tennis eight years earlier, and our friendship has grown beyond the tennis courts. He and his wife Lori have entrusted us to watch their children on numerous occasions. And we have entrusted them to be our son's God parents.

I first met my wife Tiffany at one of my college tennis matches. She shined among all of the girls watching with her long brown hair, red cheeks, and long, lean legs. My heart still beats faster every time I think of our first encounter.

Tennis might have brought the two of us together, but love held us together. It would have been very easy and understandable for Tiffany to have walked away a long time ago, having no interest in the complications created by my illnesses. She chose to stay with me, through sickness and health. And for that I am forever grateful.

It was with love that my parents tended to me in my many hours of suffering with the Crohn's disease. My mother advocated for me and was sure that I always got the best care.

And it was my father who quietly provided strength for me. Like a stake holding a tree upright, he has always stood his ground. No matter how bad the news, or how doubtful the outcome, he kept me grounded. I've always been comforted knowing that he has always been right by my side holding onto me.

And modern medicine saved my life. Thanks to diligent, dedicated scientists and doctors, I am a fortunate beneficiary of their innovations, research, and brilliance. Though a cure for Crohn's disease has not been found, the creation of Remicade has given me a quality of life that I could only have imagined ten years ago. And thirty years ago, any man diagnosed with testicular cancer was all but dead.

And the wonders of in vitro fertilization astound me. Fertility specialists gave Tiffany and me what we were told we couldn't have—a healthy baby boy. Eighteen months, forty thousand dollars, and three miscarriages later, William Dirk was born on a rainy Groundhog Day. He didn't see his shadow so he didn't head back to the hole. It was probably the best for all parties involved.

Above all, we were all gathered together because of fate. Tennis and fate saved me from the cancer.

The day I discovered the tumor, I was at a tennis match. I stood side by side with Tiffany as we watched the tennis. We stood behind the court in front of a chain-linked fence as every other ball came directly toward us.

The player on the other side of the net served. His opponent swung and missed the ball. The ball came directly at us. I didn't flinch because of the fence in front of us. As the ball approached and hit the fence, instead of deflecting off of the fence, it came right through one of the links on the fence. That tennis ball hit me square in the groin. I was immediately in agony. As I reached down to try to readjust and massage the discomfort away, I noticed something different about that testicle. It was harder and noticeably larger than the other. I immediately knew that something was very wrong. That was the beginning of my whirlwind odyssey from surgery, through chemotherapy, to the ICU, and to the edge of hell and back.

I've been involved in tennis for over twenty years. I've literally seen thousands, quite possibly millions of tennis balls hit those chain-linked fences that encompass the courts. Never before and never since have I witnessed a tennis ball literally go through a chain linked fence. Tennis balls just don't fit through those links.

Some call it luck, some call it divine intervention, I just call it fate. No matter what you call it, I guess there was just more to my game, set, life.